THE COLLEGE PROFESSOR IN AMERICA

THE COLLEGE PROFESSOR IN AMERICA

An Analysis of Articles Published in the
General Magazines, 1890-1938

CLAUDE CHARLETON BOWMAN

ARNO PRESS

A New York Times Company

New York / 1977

Editorial Supervision: MARIE STARECK

———◆———

Reprint Edition 1977 by Arno Press Inc.

Reprinted from a copy in
The Princeton University Library

THE ACADEMIC PROFESSION
ISBN for complete set: 0-405-10000-0
See last pages of this volume for titles.

Manufactured in the United States of America

———◆———

Library of Congress Cataloging in Publication Data

Bowman, Claude Charleton, 1908-
    The college professor in America.

    (The Academic profession)
    Reprint of the author's thesis, University of
Pennsylvania, 1937.
    Bibliography: p.
    Includes index.
    1. College teachers--United States. I. Title.
II. Series.
LB2331.B6 1977   378.1'2'0973   76-55170
ISBN 0-405-10001-9

THE COLLEGE PROFESSOR IN AMERICA

An Analysis of Articles Published in the
General Magazines, 1890-1938

A DISSERTATION

IN SOCIOLOGY

PRESENTED TO THE FACULTY OF THE GRADUATE SCHOOL OF THE
UNIVERSITY OF PENNSYLVANIA IN PARTIAL FULFILLMENT
OF THE REQUIREMENTS FOR THE DEGREE OF
DOCTOR OF PHILOSOPHY

CLAUDE CHARLETON BOWMAN

PHILADELPHIA
1938

To

MARY CARSON BOWMAN

TABLE OF CONTENTS

PREFACE

As one who is curious about the aspects of society that touch him directly and intimately, I have been interested in the college professor ever since my induction into the academic profession ten years ago. In the first years of my career I mulled over the significance of the attitudes and activities of my colleagues and myself for countless hours, although satisfactory answers were not always forthcoming. In the process of orientation to the academic universe I turned to the libraries. Here there were a few books on higher education but no systematic treatments of the academic profession itself. Professional educators have been concerned largely with the public schools below the college level and, indeed, those books which deal with the college and university devote scant attention to the problems of the faculty. Such material as I found was usually formal, statistical, and written in a summary fashion. Being interested primarily in the psychological aspects of social phenomena, I felt that the professor was neglected altogether or, at best, treated superficially. Perhaps to some degree this study will meet the deficiency.

It is a pleasure to acknowledge a debt of gratitude to all those who have assisted in the development of this study, although there are too many persons for specific reference. Professor Hugh Carter of the University of Pennsylvania, my adviser, deserves special mention for his valuable suggestions and kindly interest. Professor Emit Grizzell, also of the University of Pennsylvania, has given a number of suggestions on the basis of his training and experience in the field of education. The National Youth Administration merits a vote of thanks for providing a corps of assistants among whom Barney Bernstein was especially helpful. Finally, for her constant encouragement and frequent assistance I am deeply indebted to my wife, Mary Carson Bowman.

CLAUDE C. BOWMAN.

Philadelphia, Penna.
August 1, 1938.

ACKNOWLEDGMENTS

Grateful acknowledgment is made to the following publishers and authors for permission to reprint material used in this book:

The American Mercury.

D. Appleton-Century Company: *Century Magazine.*

The Atlantic Monthly Company: *Atlantic Monthly.*

Crowell Publishing Company: *The American Magazine* and *Collier's.*

The Curtis Publishing Company: *Saturday Evening Post.*

The Forum.

Harcourt, Brace and Company: *Middletown* by Robert and Helen Lynd.

Harper and Brothers: *Harper's Magazine, Life Earnings* by Harold Clark, *The Unwilling God* by Percy Marks, and *Social Mobility* by P. Sorokin.

Liberty Publishing Company: *Liberty Magazine.*

Macmillan Company: *Getting and Spending at the Professional Standard of Living* by Jessica Peixotto.

McGraw-Hill Book Company, Inc.: *Depression, Recovery and Higher Education* and *Recent Social Trends.*

The Nation.

The New Republic.

North American Review.

W. W. Norton and Company, Inc.: *The Awakening College* by C. C. Little.

Oxford University Press: *Universities: American, English, German* by Abraham Flexner.

Charles Scribner's Sons: *Scribner's Magazine, Social Organization* by Charles Cooley, and *The Protestant Ethic* by Max Weber.

Time.

The Viking Press, Inc.: *Magazine Making* by John Bakeless.

Yale University Press: *Income and Living Costs of a University Faculty* by Henderson and Davie.

INTRODUCTORY NOTE

There are a number of sources to which one may turn in studying attitudes toward, and characterizations of, the American college professor. The newspaper, the novel, the theater, and the radio constitute interesting fields for the investigation of our topic but these do not fall within the scope of the present study. Here we are dealing with magazine sources, in fact, only the general or popular magazines. The inclusion of only one medium of expression gives homogeneity to the study. Furthermore, the field has been narrowed to one type of magazine for two reasons. First, because of the enormous amount of periodical literature published in this country a selection had to be made. Second, it was deemed desirable to study magazine material which is, for the most part, written, edited, and read by non-academic persons. These too are the magazines that reach out to the greatest number of readers. Therefore only general magazines have been included, while professional periodicals for teachers have been excluded.

General magazines have not been utilized extensively as a field of sociological research but they represent an important medium for study. Articles may be ephemeral, superficial, and biased; yet, on the other hand, they are likely to be timely, interesting, and vividly human. There are many distinguished names among the contributors and even those written by less notable persons must weather the intense competition of the manuscript markets. Indeed, the artistry of composition is likely to be superior to the studied impersonality of the scientific journals. Moreover, judged by the host of new magazines and the mounting circulations of many established ones, the periodical is destined to play a greater role than ever before in America. Perhaps in many homes magazines are replacing books, for the demand in our touch-and-go life is for discussion and information that is concise. The popular expression, "make it snappy," bears witness to our impatience with prolixity.

Introduction

Table I shows the magazines and the years of their publication that fall within the scope of the analysis. However, this final list was arrived at only after considerable exploratory work. There is, for example, no agreement among librarians as to what may be classified as a "general" magazine. Also, the chronological starting-point for the investigation was uncertain at first. It was necessary to examine a number of magazines which do not appear in this table before the material for this study could be carved out of the total field. Many magazines examined could not be included because of the paucity or complete absence of relevant data. Thus, the definition of a general magazine and the chronological boundaries were not decided upon *a priori* but emerged as the work progressed.

The procedure of study consisted in a careful examination of the indexes of the bound volumes of the various magazines—unless no such indexes existed which, unfortunately, was frequently the case. In the latter event progress was very slow and various expedients were resorted to which need not be detailed here. The author would not claim that he and his assistants discovered every relevant article but he believes that the omissions are few enough to preclude any serious vitiation of the results. It was necessary to read over many articles of uncertain relevance since the titles often did not indicate the exact nature of the account. The results have been checked with Poole's Index to Periodical Literature for the decade, 1890-1899, and with the Reader's Guide to Periodical Literature for the years of the present century. It was considered advisable to make a separate examination of the sources in the absence of information concerning the adequacy of these guides. Moreover, during certain years some of the magazines were not included in them.

Since the articles could not be handled conveniently in their entirety, abstractions were made. These contained the exact words of the writers, for paraphrasing opens the door to misinterpretation. Care was exercised to avoid selection of material for abstrac-

Introduction

TABLE I

MAGAZINES ANALYZED

American Magazine	1905-1938
American Mercury	1924-1938
Atlantic Monthly	1890-1938
Century	1890-1930
Collier's	1900-1938
Forum	1890-1938
Harper's	1890-1938
Independent	1897-1928
Liberty	1925-1938
Literary Digest	1892-1938
Nation	1890-1938
New Republic	1914-1938
North American Review	1890-1938
Outlook	1895-1935
Review of Reviews	1890-1937
Saturday Evening Post	1900-1938
Scribner's	1890-1938
Time	1923-1938
World's Work	1900-1932

tion on the basis of subjective biases, although the author would be unwilling to claim that he has realized the ideal in this respect. Very probably the abstracts of another investigator going over the same field would be somewhat different. About five hundred articles were abstracted in this manner of which approximately one hundred were finally rejected as irrelevant.

What is an "article" in the present study? Magazine fiction has not been included because it is difficult to handle and difficult to determine the attitudes of the writers of fiction. The majority of the articles are of the essay type. Some are brief editorial paragraphs, others run to fifteen pages. Anonymous articles have been included, although some of these, written ostensibly by professors, have been done by professional writers in all probability. Letters to the editor have been included also.

A word concerning the form of presentation may be in order. Many quotations are used so that the author may not be charged with misinterpretation. Moreover, many of the passages give flavor to the study, for some of the writers possess an enviable ability to express themselves. Metaphors, epigrams, and anecdotes are combined into artistic wholes which cannot be adequately paraphrased. The sociological implications of the text have been developed wherever possible, care being taken, however, to differentiate clearly between the periodical *writers* and the *author* of this study. In the pages that follow those who have written the various articles are referred to as "writers" and the author of this study is referred to as the "author." The discouraging aspect of a text replete with footnotes has been partially avoided by placing periodical references at the ends of the chapters. Withal, a conscientious effort has been made to present the material in a logical and systematic manner.

CHAPTER I

THE ACADEMIC PERSONALITY

When one begins to study the material dealing with the personal characteristics of professors, it is soon apparent that it runs the gamut of feeling from romantic idealism to biting caricature. While no simple classification can be altogether adequate, it will be found convenient to make a broad dichotomy in terms of favorable and unfavorable criticisms, a few others being labelled "neutral." In making this analysis the investigator must examine the descriptive terms employed as well as the general context in order to determine whether the writer is expressing himself in a favorable or unfavorable manner.

I. FAVORABLE CHARACTERIZATIONS

Of all the favorable characterizations of the college professor, his idealism is mentioned most frequently. This is not surprising when one considers that the quest for knowledge is itself an idealistic venture. The love of knowledge is said to be characteristic of the professor; in fact, this trait may be considered an integral part of the *mores* of the academic profession.

"Most of the young men who choose academic careers are like the older ones—men of high ideals, men of studious habits, men who love knowledge and are eager in its quest, men with whom it is a joy to live if sometimes a trial to work." [1]

Harold Laski, in his penetrating manner, depicts this passion for truth that animates many academic breasts.

"Every university contains queer professors so driven by the impulse of curiosity that nothing in the world matters save the satisfaction of their hunger. They must find truth and proclaim it. Knowledge and the implications of knowledge do genuinely mean more to them than comfort or dignity or security. Like the artist and the poet and the musician, they have in them some demon which must be satisfied. . . . The old notions will not do for them; and in that private world where the most intimate part of them dwells, real revolutions occur." [2]

Indeed, there seems to be a certain element of renunciation in the life of the professor, in spite of the trend toward practicality that is mentioned by nine writers between the years 1902 and 1935. As one editor puts it:

> "Business does not allure him, nor common pleasures. He does not lust after power . . . the glories of this world seem little and remote to him . . . he is against the forces of bigness and jazz, against the temptation of mere actuality, immediacy, speed, and glitter." [3]

During the Middle Ages religious ascetics denied themselves and flagellated the flesh in order to live the life of the "spirit." The world being corrupt in their eyes, they turned away from it and spent their days in religious contemplation. There seems to be something of this same world-denying psychology in the professor. The life of the mind may be an escape from the hustle and jostle of the market-place. The intellectual life represents a type of adjustment which our more intelligent and more sensitive citizens can make to the modern world—an adjustment which may be both satisfactory and highly respectable.

Some are quite proud of this ascetic-idealistic quality.

> "So far from feeling themselves somewhat ridiculous, they are too nobly and generously proud to fight over pennies, or contend about the trappings of place and power. . . . Many of us are so unsophisticated that we dare to be frankly proud of our calling and heartily zealous in our evangel." [4]

This burst of idealism was called forth by an article in the same magazine (1914) which had excoriated the professor in America for his refusal to unionize. It sees the academic profession as the bearer of a noble tradition in the continuance of which its devotees must rise above the world, the flesh, and the devil. In this respect the professor is like the minister: each is supposed to dedicate himself to a high calling. As a matter of fact, preaching and teaching are commonly considered to be the professions farthest removed from commercialism and selfishness. One writer states that, after the ministry, teaching is the noblest, the most altruistic career. [5] An academic writer criticizes those captious individuals who constantly complain of the low salaries. There are other

values more important than the financial return, such as the satisfactions of classroom instructions. He closes with poetic fervor:

> "For with Thoreau, I hold that, if the day and night are such that I
> greet them with joy; if life emits a fragrance like sweet-scented herbs
> . . . that is my success." [6]

The professor is human. Indeed, several writers assure us that
a man may be both scholarly and human. "Many of our greatest
scholars are conspicuously broad, unassuming, sympathetic, and
human in spirit." [7] In spite of the adverse criticism heaped
upon his head, the academician is really quite a human sort of
person, insists one member of the profession.

> "The professor is human like his fellows. It may be he is too exclu-
> sive, that he mingles too little with his neighbors. . . . Still methinks, his
> humanness is not to be called into question." [8]

He goes on to suggest that, in spite of his forbidding exterior and
impassive countenance, "there beats a heart as warm as the
warmest, and dwells a spirit as young as the youngest." Perhaps
this insistence upon the human qualities of the professor indicates
that these writers are aware of a popular suspicion to the contrary.
Probably a great many people suspect the academic specialist of
having lost the common touch; in fact, every specialist is suspect
in this regard. All kinds of professional specialists may easily lose
a certain human perspective because of the circumscribed nature
of their thought and action. In their particular specialized roles,
college professors, like other occupational types, are functionaries
and not whole persons.*

However, the idealism of the profession does not stop here.
As a teacher, the professor is likely to be unselfish.

> "In its very nature the work of the teacher must be as free as possible
> from personal considerations. There is no other calling that requires such

---

* "He understood perfectly the common undergraduate idea that 'most
profs weren't human.' Like many other students, he was occasionally
startled when he realized that most of them were fathers. They must create
their children, he thought, by a mental effort." Percy Marks, *The Unwilling
God,* Harper's, 1929, p. 167.

constant practice of unselfishness as that of teaching and training the young." [9]

While there are some college teachers who seem to delight in emulating the shrewd practicality of the tradesman, there seems to be, almost inevitably, a modicum of idealism about any teacher worthy of the designation. If one is to have even a fair success in teaching, one must take some interest in the students—at least in their intellectual development. Moreover, such an interest requires imagination, that is, the ability to project oneself into the viewpoint of another. The teacher must show consideration for the immaturity of the students and the constant realization of this immaturity depends upon breadth of imagination.

This idealism may be social and abstract as well as personal and immediate. One writer asserts that there are many spheres of public activity in which professors can maintain an active interest, such as housing, public parks and recreation, and child-welfare work. [10]

All of these characterizations have been written in a complimentary spirit. The professor is human and sympathetic, loves knowledge, is unselfish, open-minded, and devoted to a noble work.

"The highest intellects, the choicest spirits of our age, may well turn to the profession of teaching for the fullest, happiest, and most rewardful work open to educated men of the country." [11]

It is important to note that the median year for these eleven articles dealing with idealism is 1913 and only one was written after 1923.

The broadening influences of the scholarly life are mentioned. The constant contact with youth is said to have a broadening effect. In general, "the chances for self-improvement and the time allowed to avail oneself of those chances are greater here than in any profession." [12] This same professorial writer defends his profession against the charge that teaching has a narrowing effect upon personality.

"The old complaint that teaching is narrowing and belittling to a man because he is dealing with immature minds is puerile. It is true only of him who is narrow and pedantic when he begins to teach. The little man becomes less as he proceeds in his gerund-grinding."

As support for the idea of the narrowing influences of teaching, it is often asserted that the growth of more and more academic specialization tends in this direction. Yet here we find refutation from a foreign-born observer.

"He must study history as a background for literature, and he will understand history only by going into political science, and politics is but a subdivision of sociology, and sociology rests on biology. . . . He must read the newspapers and the current publications in order to keep fresh and equip himself with telling illustrations from daily life for the lectures." [13]

The academic environment is conducive to such breadth. The professor has the leisure requisite to the pursuit of the cultural enjoyments that are afforded by his college or university. There are lectures of various kinds, good music, and well-educated companions. With leisure and such opportunities, it is not difficult to develop breadth along artistic and intellectual lines.

"He is cultured. If you are a scientist, he knows something about science, and has a new magazine he would like to show you. If you like music, he has been to concerts and will tell you about them; possibly he will confess humorously that he plays the violin or clarinet himself. . . . History, politics, art; he likes to talk of such things." [14]

As early as 1902 one discovers favorable comments on the newer, more practical type of college professor.

"Some Sophocles still trims his solitary lamp in every college but a newer type of professor is also everywhere in evidence: the expert who knows all about railroads, bridges, subways—practical men springing out of the new scientific and commercial energy of the nation." [15]

Not only is his knowledge of a more practical nature than formerly, but there is noted a similar trend in his general behavior. Twenty-five years ago Professor Henry S. Canby calls attention to this trend.

"The modern professor is more usually a man of the world rather than a recluse. He knows good cigars as well as good pictures and good books. He enjoys his club. . . . His talk is rarely pedantic, and far more intelligible than the dialect of the motorist or the jargon of baseball." [16]

In America such a trend is considered definitely progressive. The development of schools of business, of agriculture, and many others of the same practical nature is viewed with approbation.* Stephen Leacock, the humorist-political economist, caricatures this cult of practicality in the following passage:

> "All this is changed in America. A university professor is now a busy, hustling person, approximating as closely to a business man as he can manage to do. . . . He has a little place that he calls his 'office' with a typewriter and stenographer. Here he sits and dictates letters, beginning after the best business models, 'In re yours of the eighth ult. would say, etc.' . . . If he writes enough he will get a reputation as an executive and big things may happen to him." [17]

"Professor Antiqus" is nearly extinct, agrees Dean Max McConn, who finds four types of the "genus professor" flourishing in America. Of "Antiqus," his first type, he says,

> "This species had its most congenial habitat and flourished more abundantly at Oxford and Cambridge, and more recently in the small institutions of the United States. He is nearly extinct today, at least in the universities. It is even customary to refer to surviving specimens as being already 'fossils'." [18]

While this type is said to be losing out in the academic struggle for existence, a newer type, "Professor Uptodate-icus," is everywhere apparent. This latter type is "unquestionably a mongrel formed by an unnatural crossing of the Genus Professor with the entirely distinct genus of Business Man."

The World War is alleged to have been a factor in the development of academic practicality. A professor who had served as a captain in the army discovered through his war-time experience that "the wide, wide world was not so different from his own world, after all, and was in no wise terrifying."

> "Never again will he permit himself to think, or permit other men to say unchallenged, that the academic life is in any sense unreal or withdrawn from reality. He will not allow it to become so." [19]

---

* In Middletown it is the vocational work of the high school that wins the approval of the Rotary club. R. S. and H. M. Lynd, *Middletown*, Harcourt Brace, 1929, p. 195.

Ten years later it is asserted that the picture of the average professor as an unworldly and abstract philosopher is quite out of date.

"It would not, perhaps, be going beyond the mark to define the average academic mind of today as that of a practical man, who has, at least in the major universities, exchanged wealth and power for dignity and security." [20]

Finally, apropos of the participation of college professors in New Deal politics, Bruce Bliven makes a comparison in relation to executive competence.

"In my life I have met a great many professors; and through the accident of journalistic work it also happens that I have met and talked with perhaps eighteen of the twenty leading industrialists of the country. These great industrialists show no higher average of executive competence, in my opinion, than do an equal number of outstanding professors. What the industrialists have is stubborn egoism and lack of imagination." [21]

The professor is competent as a professional man. His abilities and inabilities as a teacher will be dealt with later, so that here we are concerned only with other aspects of the alleged competence. Not all of the discussion of this matter dates from the ascendence of the Brain Trust, for in 1902 it was said,

"In not a few important respects, the teachers in our higher institutions of learning are always better fitted by far to be counsellors and leaders of the nation than is any other class of citizens." [22]

This assertion is quite general and vague, so that we do not know exactly what public responsibilities the writer considers worthy of this competence. "Counsellors and leaders of the nation" may be anyone from a teacher to a member of the President's cabinet. Thirty years later the issue assumes more specificity, however. In the storm of encomium and diatribe that followed in the wake of Raymond Moley's appointment as Assistant Secretary of State the professor was not without his defenders. The aforementioned Bruce Bliven flatly stated his confidence in the men from the colleges and universities.

"After twenty-five years' observation of both sorts of people, I am aware of no reason why this country, or any country, cannot be run by professors as well as or better than by the masterful lords of industry." [23]

In 1934, the editorial page of *Collier's* contained a journalistic sermon entitled, "Trust Brains," from which the following excerpt is taken.

"Professors are useful because more than any other class of men they are unprejudiced or at least not prejudiced by money or business affiliations. On the matters about which they really know, their judgments are as honest and as disinterested as it is possible to find." [24]

Objectivity is a fundamental aspect of academic competence. The professor's specialty is the field of thought and thought is valuable in proportion to the freedom from bias and the openmindedness of the thinker.

"Few educated men will deny the imaginative charm that invests the existence of the solitary scholar." In the discussions of the life and personality of the college teacher the word "charm" appears frequently.

"Perhaps the real truth is that away down deep in the heart, your professor knows well that once a teacher has felt the true charm of his work, he can never find complete happiness elsewhere." [25]

Now, if the work possesses charm, perhaps we shall find that the teachers are described as charming. This is the case.

"When you meet him, you find him charming. His welcome is sunny and genial, like his smile. He plays golf and will invite you into a foursome. He plays billiards and will take you to his club, set you up to a rickey, trim you neatly, and console you like a gentleman. . . . He is always ready to play and delighted you have come." [26]

As Veblen shows in his "Theory of the Leisure Class," such behavior is characteristic of those whose wealth enables them to pursue a life of "ostentatious leisure." It requires time to cultivate charm and graciousness—time which the daily toilers do not have at their disposal for this purpose. Facility with the nuances of etiquette can be acquired only through diligent training, made possible by an existence full of leisure. This may help to explain whatever charm invests the personality of the professor, for, although the latter never becomes wealthy on an academic salary, he may possess considerable leisure in which to cultivate the social amenities.

Finally, he is described as a contented person. The contemporary world of the nineteen thirties, with its economic and political disorganization, has not been conducive to the development of this quality of mind; and it is probably not without significance that the material relevant to this point was written before the World War. In 1897 we find the following passage:

"There are a few professors, energetic men with very practical minds, who have regretted their choice, realizing that in other fields they could have tripled their incomes, but most college teachers are quite content." [27]

"Contentment" may carry a negative connotation, that is, the contented person may simply be one who is not disturbed by the disadvantages of his position. A later writer states the matter more positively.

"Many of us are so unsophisticated that we dare to be frankly proud of our calling and heartily zealous in our evangel." [28]

It is not easy to decide upon the reasons for this alleged contentment. The article from which the last quotation was taken gives two reasons:

"In the first place, the average professor has found the one well-spring of real happiness in this life, namely, a laudable and enjoyable object for his energies. And in the second place, many of them have more than a religious respect for their calling."

The aforementioned account of 1897 supplements this explanation by suggesting a number of favorable circumstances in the academic life: security of income, pleasant associates, long vacations, and contact with youth. A similar analysis is presented almost twenty years later (1916).

"He has security of tenure except in a few state universities where politics still meddle with education. He is rarely overworked . . . His associates and work are congenial. . . . He is kept in the constant companionship of youth, which is ever renewed stimulus and inspiration." [29]

As the analysis of favorable characterizations is completed, the author is impressed in two different ways. In the first place, there is a wide variety of terms utilized in these articles, signifying various aspects of the professorial personality deserving commendation. On the other hand, one is struck by conspicuous omissions. If we may believe these writers, the college professor in America is never handsome, nor eloquent, nor brilliant, nor gay. At any rate, these terms were not found, nor were their equivalents. A moment's study of these omissions will reveal that all of them refer to "spirit" or *elan*. The results of this survey of periodical literature give some verification to the criticism of a Frenchman: *"Les universites d'outre-mer n'ont pas d'esprit."*[30] Yet the personal characteristics set forth in this section of the study comprise an imposing array of desirable traits: love of knowledge, humanness, unselfishness, breadth, dispassion, practicality, competence, charm, and contentment.

II.   UNFAVORABLE CHARACTERIZATIONS

> Here he sits droning
> On some forgotten truth;
> Heedless of Springtime,
> Intolerant of youth.
>
> Here he sits dryly
> Talking all day;
> Woodenly sober
> And slim as his pay.[31]

The first fact to be recorded is that there are more articles dealing with unfavorable criticisms of the professor as a person than were found on the favorable side. Indeed, many of the articles about to be presented have been contributed by academicians. Anyone with an understanding of the objective attitude cannot help admiring the air of detachment with which professors write of their foibles.

"College professors . . . are a strange sort. No other profession in America so berates itself as does the college teacher. Imagine the osteopaths, the dentists, the bankers, the lawyers ridiculing their own practices and sacred customs in the magazines of the country in the way they . . . have been deriding college teaching. Every one who writes on the subject points out the weaknesses which most irritate him." [32]

To those who fail to appreciate self-criticism, the question will probably occur again and again: Why did these men go into such an apparently despicable profession? Or, having tasted of its bitterness, how did they resist precipitous flight into something more congenial? As a matter of fact, many have grown so habituated to the demands of social relations, which include self-assertion, rationalization, and "saving face," that they are quite incapable of appreciating the detached temper. Other professions, more intimately involved in the economic and social relationships of the community, are not likely to be very self-critical. Even those who wish to make adverse criticisms will probably use the professional journals as a medium of expression instead of the general magazines. With the academic writers about to be considered the case is otherwise. More individualistic, less influenced by *esprit de corps,* more remote from the commercial spirit, more facile with tongue and pen, such persons do not hesitate to wash the academic profession's dirty linen in public. Of course, not all of the criticisms that follow are either fair or good-humored. Personal biases and grudges apparently lead many to jump to conclusions and formulate generalizations over-hastily.

Aridity appears to be an attribute of the professorial personality, for the terms "dry" and "dull" recur frequently.

"The American professor at his best is not without a certain dry intellectual vivacity and specialized efficiency but he lacks the breadth of beam, the exuberant and contagious enthusiasm. . . .His voice has a hard professional twang, he deals himself out sparingly in social intercourse, like a commodity that may soon be exhausted." [33]

Some of the writers are not so mild as this one. A newspaper editor (Simeon Strunsky) is quite caustic.

"One of the saddest, and at the same time, one of the most instructive sights imaginable, is a college professor digging up the upper skull and lower canine tooth of a Neanderthal man. It is a contrast between growth and petrifaction, the Neanderthal man representing growth and the college professor representing petrifaction." [34]

The phrase "cold intellect" is common coin. It has often been observed that specialization in thought produces emotional desiccation, that the acquisition and dissemination of knowledge is a solemn business. How many persons are both gay and learned?

How can we account for this characteristic? A number of factors are at work and it will not be amiss to allow our contributors to assist each other in the process of explanation. For one thing, social institutions are selective and self-perpetuating.

"In American universities it is generally useless for a graduate to expect a tutorship who has not in college achieved high rank. Those, therefore, get positions who have subjected themselves to the highest pressure of the examination system." [35]

Perhaps we need to go back to the graduate school in order to see the professor in the embryonic stages. In a critical article entitled "Doctors of Dullness," one man ridicules the graduate student and his seminars.

"The tables of our university seminars are surrounded by monkish groups mulling lifelessly over stacks of hastily scribbled library cards and chanting, 'Professor Tweetzer and the recognized authorities say . . .'." [36]

The selective process in the undergraduate and graduate schools as well as the nature of graduate work seem to insure a certain amount of dullness even before the neophyte takes his place behind the desk. Once he becomes a professor it appears that still more of the juice is squeezed out. An article satirically called "The Noblest of Professions" claims that it is impossible for teaching to be noble.

"The very work of assigning lessons, hearing recitations, holding examinations, and turning in marks requires little genius and is marked by little charm. . . . The dulling tasks of the classroom have their strongest effects in ruining the mental and social life of the teacher." [37]

The college environment is said to dampen the spirit of even the most enthusiastic teachers. The following excerpt from a letter written "To a Young Man Bent on Entering the Professoriat" presents a picture not pleasant to contemplate. The counsellor is trying to show how the process of intellectual atrophy and spiritual desiccation will have advanced irrevocably after five years of professing in the classroom.

"There is nothing more deadly to a living spirit than the collegiate air. . . . You will fight against the suffocation at first with all the vigor of youth. . . . But you will give in at length and lie down conquered." [38]

The social failings of members of the collegiate fraternity are noted also. Evidently, in his social relations the professor is not all that he might be.

"Teachers show a fictitious type of bearing. Instead of open, poised frankness, they have an uneasy and uncanny reserve. . . . They have cultivated a role of omniscience and envelope themselves in a touch-me-not atmosphere. They are too unsocial . . ." [39]

The writer of this article is anonymous but is said to be a member of the profession who calls his criticisms "Confessions of a Pedagogue." Another in the same candid vein reports the strenuous efforts of himself and his friends to rid themselves of school-teacherishness by cultivating certain masculine "vices" such as smoking, drinking, and gambling. One day the writer falls into conversation with a salesman. The talk is proceeding smoothly until the salesman asks him what line of work he is doing. The writer answers that he is a teacher, whereupon a lull ensues.

" 'For a fact,' said he, 'I never would have known it.' Since this was evidently intended as a compliment, I murmured my thanks. . . . 'Don't you find,' he ventured at last, 'that you—well, that a teacher is at a—at a disadvantage with other people; that is, that other people are a—are a little afraid in the presence of a—Oh, I don't know how to put it. . . . That there is a kind of restraint?' " [40]

Recently, in a scorching indictment of the college professor, it is stated that even their wives take advantage of these social failings. All American wives, it is asserted, like to humiliate their husbands as a means of preserving their superiority over them; but the faculty wife is especially adept at deflating masculine egos.

"Faculty husbands, with that patience acquired from watching amoebas, sit quietly—or at most shift in their chairs—while their wives show what funny little fellows they are." [41]

In accounting for these failings in social intercourse, we can find a number of suggestions from the magazines. One makes the point that the nature of the intellectual life is to blame.

"The writer is a professor. . . . He is a humble member of that cloistered tribe of absent-minded and impractical bigots who strut their miserable hour apart from the haunts of life and men, fretting out lonely, sequestered existences amid the dark walls of the university or the stuffy atmosphere of the laboratory. . . . His science makes him a pedant, his much thinking . . . a mental paralytic . . . each of which characteristics becomes him ill when he forsakes his lecture-hall or laboratory and mingles upon the streets with men." [42]

Moreover, the nature of classroom relations is such that social failings easily result.

"The fit result of this habit of petty authority . . . is a stiff and surprised sheepishness in the presence of one's fellow-man. . . . Discipline and drill have been demanded of him and he has supplied these commodities to the complete satisfaction of all concerned. . . . Incidentally, to be sure, he may have stultified himself morally and intellectually, may have disqualified himself for life." [43]

The didactic habit is an integral part of the pedagogical role. The teacher may be so accustomed to teaching others that he instructs his fellows at every opportunity.

"The typical instructor feels that he is called upon to steer all courses in conversation. He is anxious to make a definite point and prove it. He cannot share in the give and take of light talk." [44]

Ordinary social intercourse calls for a certain courteous deference, a willingness, that is, to grant the plausibility of the other's attitude on the matter under discussion. There is a sympathetic ease of manner. On the contrary, the scientist, philosopher, or scholar may be sharp, critical, logical in approach, and full of his own mental processes. In a word, "teaching tends to bad manners." [45]

In addition to the environmental influences mentioned here, there seems to be a selective process that helps to explain whatever social failings are found among professors. Probably a great many persons of strongly introverted tendencies are attracted into the profession and these may be more or less inadequate in face-to-face relations. The possible correlations of temperament and occupation constitute an interesting field for social-psychological investigation. In the absence of scientific data to support the statement, we can only suggest the probability of such a temperamental selection in the academic field.

"In America there are three sexes—men, women, and professors."[46] Irritated by the lack of enthusiasm in the colleges for professional organization, this writer (1913) lashes out against the professor. He is unmanly. In plays he is depicted as guileless, innocent, and harmless.[47] A college president gives the opinion that, although his teachers are men of high ideals and studious habits, "they lack force."[48] Another writer asks, "Are Male Teachers Mollycoddles?" and concludes that an affirmative answer is not altogether unwarranted.[49] A professor, writing in 1934 under the name of George Belane, asserts that "everyone believes that professors . . . are a trifle unmanly."[50] Another makes the same comment in explaining the inertia of college faculties in regard to educational reform.

"Faculties are too cowardly and pusillanimous to create or maintain [better colleges]. We are afraid of everything and everybody, of our students and their parents, of our alumni, our friends, our trustees, our donors. We are afraid of poverty and unpopularity, of non-conformity and queerness, and, above all, many of us, of mistakes." [51]

He admits, however, that faculties are not alone in their fear. They deserve special blame only "because they have an uncommonly good chance to be men." One who has been in the teaching profession for thirty years claims to have met only seven men "who united in their individualities those qualities of manhood and that natural love of the beautiful which makes the true teacher."[52] Further, he believes that he has been more fortunate than most in his academic acquaintances. The aforementioned "George Belane" classifies college professors into four categories: the lowly creeper, the red-blooded he-man, the gold bug, and the cold intellect. The second type is not without virility but of the first he says:

"A type frequently caricatured with an apron tied around his neck, dish mop in hand, washing the dinner dishes. He is thoroughly domesticated and does well in captivity. Indeed, like the canary, he would probably perish if let loose." [53]

The characterization "unmanly" is quite naturally disparaging in a society that has been built up materially by hardy pioneers and aggressive captains of industry. Yet it is our further task to offer some explanation of the existence of this quality in the professorial personality. A recent contributor says of the professor that "sometimes he is a fugitive from reality, a tender idealist, or a disappointed minor poet."[54] Teaching may provide an escape from harsh realities. There must be thousands of sensitive persons in the country who do not adjust well to the various forms of commercial competition which demand aggressiveness and persistence.* Here again we see occupational selection at work, for teaching and the pursuit of knowledge do not require the most rugged natures. The college professor is likely to be humble, intellectually honest, and somewhat reflective, whereas our masculine ideals put a premium upon such antithetical traits as physical courage, pugnacity, and aggressiveness of an obvious sort.

Furthermore, the author would venture the opinion that the nature of academic work tends to reduce virility. Every occupation tends to mold the personalities of its members, for the daily demands of the job lead to the formation of habits and attitudes which become an integral part of the personality. In the process of adjustment to his profession, the professor may come to emphasize thought and books rather than direct action of the ordinary kind. In other words, his intellectual stature may increase at the expense of virility.†

Closely related to unmanliness is the charge that he is impractical. The absent-minded professor living a cloistered existence among a multitude of books has long been a popular stereotype in America. Students, business men, and alumni write about this trait; professors themselves make mention of this criticism but only as representing the opinion of others. One college teacher, for example, tells of the attitude of a bank teller.

---

* "A man without a persistent character, in spite of his talent, cannot become either a great scientist, or money-maker, or ruler, or inventor, or leader generally. . . . In vain would one try to find among great political rulers, or the captains of industry . . . 'soft', sentimental, human, timid, sincere, and entirely honest natures." P. Sorokin, *Social Mobility,* Harpers, 1927, p. 309.

† Note that many of the characteristics called "idealistic," from a favorable point of view, are considered "unmanly" here.

"He could unbend toward me as one softens to a care-free child. I was one who lived apart from the machinery of business, supplying it, as it were, an occasional meager drop of oil. . . . 'Naughty, naughty,' he seemed to say, 'mustn't touch' when I ventured a remark on the condition of the street. . . . I think that he pictured me as one likely to boil my watch and time it with an egg, or to pat my own child's head on the street and say, 'Whose little boy are you?' "[55]

A business man is quoted as saying:

"I get along with all sorts of men except the occasional professor that I meet, the kind of a man who thinks that life is got out of books. . . . He doesn't know how to do anything. He thinks it's enough to read books and to say things and to talk about generalities."[56]

Similarly, a former college teacher who went into business expresses himself on this point.

"I have often wondered why professors were so frequently held in contempt by business men and scorned by the laboring classes. The reason is clear to me now. Many a teacher, instead of putting himself in the way of humanity, withdraws into the comparative quiet and detachment of the university quadrangle."[57]

Students give utterance to the same attitude. Twenty-five years ago an undergraduate stated that faculty members are unfit to pursue any other line of work.[58] A foreign-born student was deeply shocked at the irreverence displayed toward the faculty in his college. A friend assured him that professors were not red-blooded but led cloistered lives amid second-hand experiences.

". . . if they had been made of the proper stuff, they would have gone in for big things, for a kind of work that matters in the world, instead of peddling away their lives over little text-books and specimens and kids' themes."[59]

Many of the alumni may have the same view. A group of them are talking about their professors.

"But you take these professors—what practical knowledge of life have they got? Half of them are parlor Bolsheviks. . . . Sure, it's all theory with them . . ."[60]

Finally, apropos of the recent accession of a few academic men to political power in the early days of the New Deal, it is suggested that the absent-minded, highly abstract, impractical gentleman of learning is a reality but that his numbers are not legion.

"Everyone has known a teacher or two of whom these words are a literal description, but they are rare exceptions. Strangely enough, however, something of this taint still clings to the cap and gown, no matter who wears it." [61]

Another magazine echoes this sentiment, asserting that the stereotype is a good deal of an imaginary set-up. Just as all Scotchmen are not so thrifty as the funny papers indicate, so the professor is not always "so absurdly absent-minded, or impractical, or theoretical, or generally unworldly as the funny columns suggest." [62]

Nevertheless the criticism cannot be evaded, especially in this country. Here those who show an indisposition for all types of activity except those of an intellectual or artistic nature are likely to be frowned upon. Our practical interests flow from the capitalistic spirit which Max Weber has defined as "the idea of a duty of the individual toward the increase of his capital, which is assumed as an end in itself."* In the ethically sanctioned struggle for gain, the "practical" man will not be beguiled by learning or philosophical reflection for these cannot be turned into cash readily. So it comes about that those devoted to the things of the mind are criticized as "impractical." Thus, the classic indictment of the arch-satirist, George Bernard Shaw, is quoted with approval: "Those who can, do; those who can't, teach." The sociologist understands that this statement owes its effectiveness to the values of practicality current here.†

The academic man is accused of being over-critical and over-analytical. The critical spirit is one of the foundation-stones of the intellectual life, so that it is not surprising that some should be charged with possessing virtue in excess. It is not strange that the full-fledged professor shows this trait at times, in view of the

---

* Max Weber, *The Protestant Ethic* (tr. by Talcott Parsons) Scribner's, 1930, p. 51.

† A colleague who spent the first twenty years of his life in Norway stated that he never heard the Shavian indictment of the teaching profession until he came to America.

training obtained in the graduate school. G. Stanley Hall, forty years ago, painted the following picture of graduate work:

> "In intellectual work he does not find companionship either warm or large. . . . He brings his most cherished convictions and ideals to a mart where others just as sacred and cherished are diverse and even contradictory. . . . If he takes a course in the history of philosophy, and finds views to which his soul goes out, the next system overturns them and he concludes that it is better to hold no opinions. . . . He has lost the flavor of conviction, and, if he has not positive ill health, he is a moral valetudinarian. . . . Like the Romans in the old days when all creeds were tolerated, he feels that all things are alike true and alike false, while his heart is growing cold and his head gray in vain." [63]

Reinhold Niebuhr tells of a friend whom he calls an unhappy intellectual because of the frustrations born of skepticism.

> "While my friend thus sacrifices everything for the principle of freedom, he has fallen into a complete moral skepticism in every other respect. He laughs at values which men call good and evil. Nothing is really good or evil if you are intelligent enough to make a complete analysis of its character." [64]

It is the task of the psychoanalyst to determine whether a good deal of such thinking is not cynicism masking as the critical spirit. This same "unhappy intellectual" is further described as one who sees monogamy resting upon irrational taboos and thus ridiculous, politics are too coarse to be tolerated, patriotism only causes conflict and war, business is organized banditry, and religious faiths are the fantastic illusions of children. The writer considers his friend biased because "having discovered that all motives are mixed, he lets his mind dwell upon the ignoble rather than the noble portions of the mixture."* The article concludes with a critical comment upon analytical intelligence.

> "He mistakes analytic intelligence for wisdom. He does not see that the poet and the artist and the prophet have an imaginative grasp of reality which is no less intelligent than that of the pure analyst. . . . They regard life telescopically rather than microscopically."

---

* It is here that the prejudicial nature of such thinking reveals itself, for the analyses are consistently pessimistic, representing a kind of dignified grumbling.

Teaching may conduce to a hypercritical attitude. It is part of the teacher's function, in the ordinary school, to discover the faults and mistakes of the pupils. This can easily lead to a loss of human sympathy. The teacher tends to insist upon details and to analyze everything to atoms. Learning is formalized "till all the juice is squeezed out and nothing but mentally indigestible fiber remains."[65] The author suggests that the marking system also tends to develop the critical attitude of the pedagogue. For the most part, marking papers or recitations is a matter of ascertaining how incorrect they are. One hundred percent is perfect and the teacher's task is to figure out how far short the students fall.

Moreover, the professor is called unwholesome.

"What are the worst things that the world can say about us? We are pedantic, oracular, academic. We are not healthy, normal, lovable human beings. We have too many nerves and too few muscles; too many spectacles and tomes; too few sunbeams and first-hand adventures."[66]

A little exercise and fresh air might ease many of the tribulations of the academic life. Those engaged in mental labor run the hazard of disturbing the healthy balance between the mind and the body. They become too "heady." While there are probably a few golf enthusiasts on every faculty, many have a tendency to exercise only the muscles of the eyes and throat.

Is there any originality among college professors? The absence of creative ability is voiced more than once in the periodicals. It would seem that there is a sterile quality about the professorial mind, if we can believe some of the writers. At the close of the last century Bliss Perry stated this view with regard to his own field.

"Very little good creative literature comes from universities. There is a sophisticated sense that everything has been written, and written better than it is likely to be written again."[67]

This lack of originality is sometimes expressed by asserting that professors are too conventional, as in the following passage:

"The professor is bound by tradition and precedent; he is a slave to books, to conventionality. . . . He is afraid to venture beyond the establised boundaries . . . he is too timid to launch his bark upon the uncharted seas . . .

he is sadly lacking in originality and initiative; he dares affirm nothing for which he cannot cite chapter and verse. . . . He is a parrot, not a prophet; he distrusts the present, dreads the future, is at home only in the past." [68]

A recent contributor considers this matter to be of first importance for the cause of higher learning in America. The man "groping for new paths, advancing thoroughly heterodox ideas" is discouraged at every turn.[69]

Why is he discouraged and by whom? It is suggested that "institutions have always been the foes of progress."[70] Certainly we must take into account the nature of social institutions. Formalism tends to settle upon every institution—the family, the church, the school, business, and government. Having acquired a definite organization in the past, there is inertia with respect to change. The leaders of institutionalized activities are "vested interests" who, because of their positions of power under the *status quo,* may resist attempts at change. For the mass of followers the traditional ways have become their ways, that is, the *mores* are their own habits and attitudes. Thus, institutions rather easily develop an inflexibility of structure and of purpose, confuse means and ends, and fail to meet new needs. One of the indices of "ossification" (E. A. Ross' term) is the suppression of the creative spirit. "Too much mechanism in society . . . interferes with growth and adaptation . . . suppresses individuality and stupefies or misdirect the energies of human nature."* The author sees no reason to except the colleges and the professors from this general interpretation. The adjustment which the majority of professors make to the educational system insures a conservative outlook. Accordingly, those who recommend novel procedures are called visionary or indecorous, while the *mores* are rationalized according to a pattern well known to sociology, particularly since the days of W. G. Sumner. In the face of such resistance only courageous nonconformity can hope to be effective. Yet if the academic gospel "is one of conduct, not of adventure, and of safe conduct at that"[71] we begin to understand the alleged lack of originality. Of course,

---

* Charles H. Cooley, *Social Organization,* Scribner's, 1909, p. 342.

the self-same fear of change and of advocating change is characteristic of the majority of people in any society. The sole justification
for singling out the professor for special criticism is that his work
calls for a spirit of openmindedness and freedom.

Another reason given for the scant flowering of creative abilities among the faculty concerns the whole issue of academic freedom. Administrative control of our universities is said to smother
originality.

"It is curious how little attention has been given to the smothering effect
of such administrative control in American institutions of higher learning." [72]

This writer goes on to say that the universities have not been
molded by such men as Veblen and Dewey, Beard and Commons
but rather by "humdrum minds with so-called 'administrative'
ability, men who conceived it as their highest ambition to become
a dean or a president rather than to excel in thought or writing."
And what happens when this type of professor succeeds in his
ambitions? Professor Laski answers as follows:

"When the academic politician becomes a university president, there is
nothing he subconsciously fears as a genuinely inventive mind." [73]

Finally, an attitude of receptivity may preclude the expression
of original ideas. "Sometimes an overaccumulation of material
keeps scholars from writing."[74] The creative spirit is not fos-
tered by too great an addiction to books. Men of originality may
be inveterate readers but their reading is not carried on in an
attitude of acquiescence. On the other hand, college professors
may come to lean so heavily upon their libraries that creative intelligence atrophies through neglect.

Not content with the tar and feathers added up to this point,
several call the belabored professor lazy.

"Most college professors are incurably lazy. Since the days of Socrates,
greatest of them all, they have been men who preferred talking to the
greater ardors of writing or action. Some of them, having worked pretty
hard in their student days collecting Phi Beta Kappa keys and writing
dissertations, seem forever after to be left in a state of chronic fatigue." [75]

This writer tells of the advice given by a professor to a friend of his. The first year or two you have to work pretty hard getting lectures in shape, said the older academician. Then you ought to write a text-book which, of course, you will require the students to buy; and then for the next twenty years it's easy sailing. Another critic agrees with this attitude. The under-paid professor is a myth; indeed, most of them get more than they deserve.

"They never actually teach more than fifteen hours a week and that is exceptional. In the undergraduate institutions they teach the same courses year in and year out, using their old notes and old jokes. . . . When this is pointed out to them, they complain about the hours of preparation. . . . That is all very impressive . . . but sheer nonsense." [76]

This completes the survey of the psychological diseases of the academic profession. While no attempt has been made to quote every unfavorable remark, the chief ones have been described and interpreted sociologically (with the assistance of the writers themselves). The professor is called dull, socially, inadequate, unmanly, impractical, over-analytical, unwholesome, conventional, and lazy. Again, the omissions may be noted. No one has impugned his moral integrity. Whatever animadversions may be heaped upon his learned head, one cannot successfully maintain, on the basis of a study of the general magazines, that the professor is immoral. May he find consolation in virtue.

REFERENCES

[1] *World's Work,* I, 173, 1900.
"Are Young Men's Chances Less?" Two College Presidents.

[2] *Harper's,* CLVIII, 391, 1929.
"The Academic Mind," Harold Laski.

[3] *Nation,* CXV, 653, 1923.
"Americanism," Ed.

[4] *Forum,* LI, 321, 1914.
"The Professorial Quintain," F. B. R. Hellems.

[5] *World's Work,* XXII, 14560, 1911.
"Blending Business and Scholarship."

[6] *Atlantic Monthly,* XCVIII, 368, 1906.
"Confessions of an Obscure Teacher."

[7] *Nation,* XCVII, 433, 1913.
Letter to the Editor.

[8] *Century,* XCIX, 404, 1920.
"The Perplexities of a Professor," by Himself.

[9] *Review of Reviews,* LX, 339, 1919.

[10] *Atlantic Monthly,* LXXXIX, 1902.
"The College Professor and the Public," Bliss Perry.

[11] *Cosmopolitan,* XXXV, 92, 1903.
"Choice of a Teaching Profession," Reverend Mackenzie.

[12] No. 5 above.

[13] *Century,* XCV, 376, 1918.
"The Tired College Man," M. E. Ravage.

[14] *American Mercury,* II, 1924.
"Pedagogue: Old Style," James Cain.

[15] No. 9 above.

[16] *Harper's,* CXXVI, 782, 1912.
"The Professor," Henry S. Canby.

[17] *Harper's,* CXLIV, 741, 1921.
"Oxford As I See It," Stephen Leacock.

[18] *Nation,* CXIII, 537, 1921.
"The Genus Professor," Max McConn.

[19] *Scribner's,* LXV, 465, 1919.
"The Professor and the Wide, Wide World," Gordon H. Gerould.

[20] *Harper's,* CLVIII, 391, 1929.
"The Academic Mind," Harold Laski.

[21] *New Republic,* LXXVI, 11, 1933.
"Washington Kaleidoscope," Bruce Bliven.

[22] *Forum,* XXXIII, 1902.
"Degradation of the Professorial Office," G. T. Ladd.

[23] No. 20 above.

[24] *Collier's,* May 19, 1934.
"Trust Brains," Ed.

[25] No. 8 above.

[26] No. 14 above.

[27] *Scribner's,* XXII, 512, 1897.
"The Life of a College Professor," Bliss Perry.

[28] No. 3 above.

[29] *Scribner's,* LX, 639, 1916.
"Lo, the Poor Professor."

[30] *Atlantic Monthly,* CLVII, 236, 1936.
"Blind Alleys," Carl Friedrich.

[31] *American Mercury,* VIII, 16, 1926.
"Professeur," Maurice Kelly.

[32] *Outlook and Independent,* CLI, 326, 1929.
"Utopia College," Addison Hibbard.

[33] *Nation,* XCIV, 52, 1912.
"Personality in the Professor," Editorial.

[34] *Harper's,* CXLV, 764, 1922.
"The Shame of Health," Simeon Strunsky.

[35] *Atlantic Monthly,* XLV, 594, 1880.
"The Examination System in Education," Willard Brown.

[36] *North American Review,* CXV, 228, 1929.
"Doctors of Dullness," H. W. Whicker.

[37] *Bookman,* XXII, 637, 1905.
"The Noblest of Professions," H. W. Boynton.

[38] *Atlantic Monthly,* CXXXVII, 320, 1926.
"To a Young man Bent on Entering the Professoriat," Geo. Boas.

[39] *Scribner's,* XLIII, 476, 1908.
"Confessions of a Pedagogue."

[40] *Atlantic Monthly,* CXIV, 127, 1914.
"In Those Days," Robert M. Gay.

[41] *Harper's,* CLXVIII, 458, 1934.
"Faculty Wives," George Belane.

[42] No. 8 above.

[43] No. 37 above.

[44] No. 39 above.

[44] *World's Work,* XVI, 10308, 1908.
"Are Male Teachers Mollycoddles?"

[46] *Forum,* L, 445, 1913.
"The Third American Sex," George C. Cook.

[47] *Scribner's,* LXII, 251, 1917.
"The Guileless Professor."

[48] No. 1 above.

[49] No. 45 above.

[50] No. 41 above.

[51] *Nation,* CXXII, 576, 1924.
"A Dream of a Narrow College," Henry Mussey.

[52] *Scribner's,* LXXXV, 217, 1929.
"The Spirit of the Game," H. W. Whicker.

[53] *Harper's,* CLXVIII, 552, 1934.
"Faculty Husbands," George Belane.

[54] *Forum,* XCIII, 226, 1935.
"Professors have a Cinch," Dixon Wecter.

[55] *Atlantic Monthly,* CXXI, 218, 1918.
"Why Teach?" Robert M. Gay.

[56] No. 5 above.

[57] *Harper's,* CXL, 249, 1920.
"Why I Remain in Industry," by "Doctor of Philosophy."

[58] No. 33 above.

[59] No. 13 above.

[60] *Harper's,* CLIII, 652, 1927.
"Education," Lee W. Dodd.

[61] *Atlantic Monthly,* CLII, 124, 1933.
"The Professor's Dilemma," "Scrutator."

[62] *Saturday Evening Post,* CCVI, 1933.
"Government by Professors," Albert W. Atwood.

[63] *Forum,* XVII, 1894.
"Scholarship and the Training of Professors," G. Stanley Hall.

[64] *Atlantic Monthly,* CXLIII, 483, 1929.
"The Unhappy Intellectuals," Reinhold Niebuhr.

[65] No. 39 above.

[66] *Survey,* XXXV, 249, 1915.
"What Ails the Teacher?" Elizabeth Hodgson.

[67] No. 27 above.

[68] *Nation,* CVIII, 751, 1919.
"The Education of a Professor," J. Ritchie Smith.

[68] No. 30 above.
[70] No. 34 above.
[71] No. 51 above.
[72] No. 30 above.
[73] No. 20 above.
[74] No. 27 above.
[75] No. 54 above.
[76] No. 41 above.

Oh, see the man, a funny dresser,
He's just an English 2 professor.
The palm beach suit, you all remember,
He wore it last year till November.
He is so old and likewise thin
That you can see where his socks begin.
What hair he has he never brushes,
The hat he wears, ye Gawds, what crushes.
No wonder he's so weak and thin,
No square meal does he have within;
But he eats sandwiches and tea
(He has to, with his salary).[1]

CHAPTER II

Salary and Academic Life

I. SALARY

This bit of collegiate doggerel is hardly poetry but the pages which follow may suggest that it contains some degree of truth. Whatever the joys of the academic life, the magazines do not create the impression that America has been prodigal with her professors in the matter of dollars and cents. However, let us turn to the data.

Are Academic Salaries Adequate?

One of the earliest accounts is given by President Harper of the University of Chicago in 1893. On the basis of a study of more than one hundred institutions of higher learning he found that the general average for a year of academic services was about $1470. The bare figure is not significant in itself so that some comparisons are made. The salaries of the lower class of professors compare with the wages of the skilled workmen in the mechanical industries. The salaries that range upward from the general average compare with the pay of the lower grades of responsible clerical and subordinate administrative employes. It is only the highest class of college professors who are to be compared with the lower grades of responsible officers of a railroad, industrial corporation, or insurance company.

"There is practically no class of college professors whose pay is on a level with the pay of men in positions of first or second rank and responsibility in the industrial community; and yet no one questions that the higher grades of university work require quite as exceptional gifts and quite as elaborate preparation, together with all the most desirable traits of character that go to make up the highest efficiency in the front ranks of the industrial life. For the employment of equally rare and indispensable talents, in equally exacting and responsible positions, the teachers in our universities are paid at a rate that will in no wise compare with first-rate salaries or personal incomes in mechanical industry or in the professions."[2]

39

President Harper recommended that there should be increases in the salaries of not less than fifty percent, which would have raised the general average to $2000, the most highly paid men from $4000 to $7000. This recommendation, he states, is only a matter of simple justice and "that it would also be from the broadest point of view a genuine economy may be taken for granted."

This next account and, in fact, many subsequent ones are more impressionistic than the one just given but nevertheless present a picture of financial difficulties common to a large number. A young man went to college, made out reasonably well, and decided that he would be a scholar. He borrowed fifteen hundred dollars to take graduate courses, got married on the delusion that two could live as cheaply as one, and at twenty-five, thus encumbered—from a financial standpoint—began his life as a college professor. He accepted a position in a small college with the idea of moving on to greater things as soon as he paid off his debts, got some experience, and saved some money. This was in 1882. At the time of writing (1897) he was still at the same college. During the first eight years he had rid himself of the debt, acquired two children, a maid, and a $2000 salary. Scholarly ambitions of the first order had vanished; he was satisfied to be "just a professor." [3]

Evidence that the plight of this academician is not atypical comes from an article in *Scribner's* published in the same year. The salary of a full professor is said to be a little over $2000, with $3000 being paid in the big universities. A few may get upwards of $4000 but these are so scarce that their incomes hardly affect the general average.[4] Several years later *World's Work* tells of a growing volume of discussion about professors' salaries. While a man at Harvard may earn as much as $5000, at Yale $3750, the man growing gray in a small college that pays only $1200 to $1800 is very much more common. He is unable to save for old age or to educate his children.

"Such colleges must continue to accept third and fourth rate men unless the weaker institutions will unite or America can produce an enormous crop of philanthropists." [5]

Of course, averages do not tell the story in sufficient detail. What was happening at this time was the employment of an increasing number of instructors to handle the work of the classroom and their low salaries began to pull down the averages. The salaries of the full professors had not declined but the inclusion of a greater proportion of instructors accounted for the fact that "in one of our largest universities the average ten years ago was $1500; it is now only $1257. In another one, the average was $1454 and now it is $1355." [6]

The following type is not unknown to the campus though his numbers have probably dwindled during the last three decades. This writer analyzed the itemized household accounts which his wife had kept for the previous nine years (1896-1905) during which time he had been connected with one of the large and wealthy universities. Two years were spent as instructor, two as assistant professor, and the next five as associate professor. His economic story can be told very simply. The average annual expenditure was $2794; the average salary, $1328. For the privilege of teaching he had paid the difference, or $1466 annually, from private means.* He goes on to suggest that on the basis of his own analysis and of experiences of colleagues the professor's salary should be increased sixty percent.

"Large salaries, commensurate with what equal ability would bring in other lines of work ($10,000 to $50,000) might be just, but would be undesirable, as they would tend to serve as bait to attract mercenary and lower types of men. . . . But a man fit to occupy a chair in a university should be paid enough to enable him to live in decency and comfort, . . . retiring in old age to something other than absolute penury." [7]

The author has no means of ascertaining the number of college trustees who subscribed to the *Atlantic Monthly* in 1905 but a careful perusal of this writer's tables of household expenses would undoubtedly have opened their eyes to the financial realities of the faculty. In face-to-face relations college administrators and

---

* Jessica Peixotto found only five out of ninety-six cases studied at the University of California "whose vested income largely exceeds salary." *"Getting and Spending at the Professional Standard of Living,* Macmillan, 1927, p. 253.

teachers exhibit a definite reticence in regard to money matters; it seems incompatible with the dignity and monastic idealism of the profession. However, in the anonymity of the popular journal— this writer gives his initials only—the embarrassing details are poured out in profusion.

By 1907 the average salary was said by President Schurman of Cornell to be $1500, the maximum seldom being more than $3000 to $4000. This income, he pointed out, was far below that of engineers, lawyers, and physicians. "Indeed, the salaries of professors have remained practically stationary for two decades while the cost of living has increased about fifty percent." [8] The time has come, he said, when benefactors can perform the greatest service not by devoting their money to buildings and material equipment but to strengthening the teaching force. About this same time the *Literary Digest* published an abstract of a pamphlet which had been issued by the Carnegie Foundation for the Advancement of Teaching. Its statistics were as follows:

"The average salary of a full professor in the one hundred leading institutions varies from $1350 to nearly $4800, the average being somewhere near $2500. . . . An American teacher who has gone through college, taken a post-graduate course, and prepared himself for the profession of teaching may hope to obtain at the age of twenty-eight a salary of $1250, at thirty-one $1750, at thirty-three $2250, and at thirty-five—at which age the able man will have gained his professorship—a salary of $2500." [9]

Certain comparisons with German universities are presented also. While the German professor had far greater financial and social reward than his American colleague, greater security, and fuller protection for old age and for his wife, it must not be forgotten that his income prior to the election to a chair (at about forty years of age) is pitifully meager.

In 1919 President Hibben of Princeton asserted that retail prices of food had risen about eighty percent since 1915 and that "in the last five years the pay of school and college teachers has advanced only a meager fraction, in many cases not at all." [10] He further calls attention to the significance of the fruits of patient research of devoted scientists, for which they receive no compensation.

The professors of physics, chemistry, or engineering who perfect inventions or make notable discoveries cannot patent them or commercialize them without losing caste. "Many fortunes have been made—for others—by the labors of college professors." In particular during the war, tremendous contributions were made by university faculties.

In a satirical vein a professor sets forth his financial problem. He claims to have received the following letter.

"My dear Professor A,

I have the good fortune to inform you on behalf of the trustees that, at a formal meeting held this morning, it was unanimously agreed to raise your salary from its present figure, $1800, to $1900. The Board was led to this action, my dear sir, quite as much in recognition of your faithful and efficient service as in consequence of the rather considerable increase in the cost of living within the past two or three years.

> Believe me, my dear sir,
> Your humble servant,
> X................" [11]

He then goes on to show how his return on the investment in his education has been ridiculously inadequate and asks what annual return would a practical business man expect from such an investment. "How does the investment of a hod-carrier compare?" Yet he denies any desire to leave the profession, for his work is a sort of passion.

Shortly after the World War we find a number of articles dealing with salary, for the high cost of living was discovering the professor to be especially vulnerable. Trevor Arnett of the General Education Board stated in 1921,

"The colleges have made earnest efforts to hedge the gap between the meager salaries and the increased cost of living. Yet the replies to the questionnaires show the rise in salary on the average amounted in 1920 to only twenty to thirty-five percent of the other increase." [12]

This professional penury had led Mr. John D. Rockefeller in 1919 to offer $50,000,000 toward a nation-wide movement to pay college teachers more adequately.

Yet even this gigantic contribution to professorial welfare did not solve the problem altogether and we find the *Literary Digest* a few years later (1927) making some comparisons within the teaching field.

"In New York City the teachers of grammar-school grades receive more than the highest paid full professors in two-thirds of the colleges. . . . Only one college in thirty pays teachers a maximum, three out of ten do not pay as much as elementary teachers get in their sixth year, and one out of three colleges pays seasoned instructors less than New York pays to its beginning teachers." [13]

In the same year this same publication reported President Angell of Yale as asserting that many college professors get paid less than the chauffeurs of the men whose sons they teach. The Yale drive for $20,000,000 is to be, it further reports, almost wholly for the reconstruction of salaries.

"Dr. Angell has pointed out that the teaching salaries at Yale are only fifty percent above the 1913 average while the cost of living is seventy-eight percent higher." [14]

Yale University, however, cannot be taken as representative of the country as a whole. While Yale professors appear to be in a worse plight in 1927 than in 1913, a further study by Mr. Arnett does not substantiate this conclusion for the country as a whole.*

The periodicals included in this study furnish no statistical data on salary trends during the depression of the thirties. A college president writing in the *New Outlook* in 1932 does, however, comment upon what he chooses to call "The Crisis in the Ph. D." After picturing the opportunities and advantages of the profession in the salad days of industrial expansion, he turns to the other side of the medal.

"The boom of higher education began to collapse with the collapse of the boom in stocks and bonds. . . . Incomes from endowments that depended as much on the value of securities as the fortunes of the donors were

---

*

	Nominal Averages	Real Averages
1914-15	$1724	$1724
1919-20	2279	1114
1926-27	2958	1825

General Education Board, "Teachers' Salaries," 1928 p. 18.

drastically cut. . . . Millionaires were disappearing everywhere and their philanthropy passed with them. . . . This collapse in higher education has resulted in great deflation in the teaching field. Finding a job no longer presents any of the earlier simplicity and comparative ease. . . . Pay cuts have taken place in all but the wealthiest universities. Many institutions . . . have taken to scrip. . . . Classes have been doubled and trebled to allow for a small staff. Extra work has been sought by hundreds of faculties in the effort to eke out vanishing incomes. And hundreds have been laid off." [15]

He goes on to state that vacancies are not being filled, that many professors hesitate to take a sabbatical leave for fear their places will not exist when they return, and that much of the charm and ease has departed from academic life. Practical-minded, he asserts that "the consolations of the mind are a poor substitute for material well-being, and an intellectual in doubt about his next meal is in no better shape than a homeless worker." Unfortunately, he states, the graduate-student enrollment has not shrunk in any way comparable to the shrinkage in college jobs.

"The few opportunities that occur are pursued with devastating competition. One vacancy in a Pacific coast college was sought by four hundred applicants. All of them were supported with the best of references, and all were willing to do any amount of work at any rate of pay. Department heads in some of the larger universities have thrown academic reserve to the winds and are writing to the smaller places to ask if they can take one or two men this year. The answer is, No."

Two years later Oswald Villard urged the professors to organize a union in the interest of determining minimum wages for the profession.

"If the President thinks it necessary to fix a minimum wage for mine workers and factory workers . . . why not a living minimum wage for college professors? . . . Above all, college teachers ought now to organize in unions, following the example of editorial writers and reporters. . . . Mr. Roosevelt declares that he is freeing industry from innumerable shackles. Why not strike a few from the wrists of university professors?" [16] *

---

* The most exhaustive study of the effects of the depression upon the academic profession is that of Committee Y of the American Association of University Professors. A few excerpts from this report are relevant at this point. *(Continued on next page.)*

The periodicals give special attention to the financial plight of
the young man in the academic profession because his budgetary
problems are particularly acute. In 1909 the *Nation* editorialized
on "Instructors' Wages," basing its comment upon a study just
completed.

> "Poorly remunerated as the professor still is, his salary has been slowly
> approaching its proper size, but the instructor has dropped so far that in
> purchasing power, the average teacher of 1908 is but sixty to seventy per-
> cent as well off as was his colleague of twenty years ago. At Johns Hopkins
> the average instructor now receives $725 a year, at Brown $734, at most
> other colleges nearly $1000, and sometimes a little more." [17]

It is shown further that the numbers in this rank have increased
much more rapidly than the higher ones, so that, as a result, in-

---

"The common assumption that large numbers of college teachers have
been released from employment since the onset of the depression does not
appear tenable." Page 31.

"The foregoing analysis of salary reductions and restorations reveals
certain clear tendencies. In all but 16.0 percent of the colleges, universities,
and teachers colleges for which the committee had data the reductions
were introduced at some time between the years 1930-1931 and 1935-1936
and were concentrated in the years 1932-1933 and 1933-1934. The public
and western institutions were most sensitive, and the public institutions
tended to impose larger reductions than those privately endowed. . . .
Employment conditions within the profession have definitely turned upward,
about two years after the general business upturn. . . . In terms of salaries,
less than half of the institutions making cuts have as yet moved in the
direction of restorations . . . faculty members must expect to find the
improvement in their own conditions, in terms of salary and employment,
lagging somewhat behind the general business curve." Pages 49-50.

Nevertheless, other professions suffered greater losses during the depression than did the academic group. Cf. Pages 50-52.

Depression, Recovery and Higher Education, McGraw-Hill Book Co., 1937.

Another study that may be cited at this point encompassed fifty-one land-
grant institutions:

	Nominal Salaries		Real Salaries (a)
	1929	1934	1934
Professors	$4457	$3775	$4754
Associate Professors	3349	2903	3656
Assistant Professors	2818	2449	3084
Instructors	2060	1769	2228

a—Figures in this column were computed by the author from cost of
living indexes (1929 = 100).

Salaries in Land-Grant Colleges, U. S. Office of Education, Circular No.
157, Feb., 1936.

structors and assistants comprise one-half or even two-thirds of
many a faculty. How can we expect enthusiastic teaching so long
as "scholars have to work until well past thirty for the wages of a
New York street sweeper?" In the same year the same periodical
inveighed against this circumstance in another editorial. After
depicting how the young academician is caught between a heavy
teaching load and the necessity to turn out research work in order
to get ahead, the salary situation is taken up. The instructor who
is married must live in a constant state of anxiety which naturally
precludes full attention to intellectual endeavors.

"One thousand dollars will indeed furnish food and shelter of a certain
kind but it is, frankly speaking, foolish for an instructor with a family to
attempt to live on such an income. The inevitable result is that instructors
are forebearing in greater number every year to marry at all, or else they
have few or no children. An early marriage or a fair-sized family is openly
regarded in university circles as a serious indiscretion." [18]

This editorial writer claims that the salaries of full professors are
at least three times that of an instructor on first appointment and
often four or five times as much. This becomes even more unfair
when we consider that the older and more distinguished men have
many more opportunities for "extras" from lecturing, royalties,
and investments. Such inequalities in opportunities have been
found by several investigators.*

After the war a professor tells how industries are looking to the
universities for scientific men and are offering them tempting
remunerations. If the schools are to withstand this new competition, he asserts, they must bind their men to greater loyalty by
raising their salaries.

"It is fair to assert as a prophecy, not as a warning, that the universities
of America must give proper aid to their younger men without delay if they
would avoid demoralization of instruction and research. At last, outside
interests are bidding openly for all, not part, of the time of university
teachers." [19]

---

* Miss Peixotto states that "between the period of instructorship and that
of full professorship, the faculty member's gains from outside work apparently increase." op. cit. page 89-90.

In 1921 a periodical published the results of a study of salaries at Vassar and the instructors' were found to range from $1200 to $1800 a year—less than the average mechanic's wage. "These facts are not new and the moral has always been obvious." [20]

The depression of the thirties brought forth further remarks on the plight of the young professor. Again the *Nation* champions the cause of the lesser lights of the campus.

"A large proportion of the necessary economy in operating expenses inevitably has had to fall upon the salaries of university instructors. . . . By far the greatest number of those who have lost their jobs are instructors and part-time assistants. . . . In nearly every case the people most severely affected by the retrenchment are those least able to stand it. A professor can readjust his scale of living to eighty percent of his former salary much more easily than an instructor can get along on the absolute minimum. . . . To show conclusively how those in the higher ranks have remained relatively secure at the expense of the 'smaller fry,' I quote from the report on 'The Economic Condition of the Profession in 1932.' " [21] *

A writer in the *Forum* minces no words about the matter. She (perhaps the wife of an instructor) speaks of the "horrors of insecurity" that can be understood only by those on the inside— "to say nothing about actual poverty."

"On the whole, the young professor who has not married a rich wife and who has been foolhardy enough to have a family will find himself in an exceedingly difficult situation if he tries to live the normal life of a responsible individual in his class in our society. Too often he will find the situation baffling beyond solution unless some *deus ex machina* intervenes. But divine interventions are rare; and the man who can do himself justice as a teacher while he is wondering where the next meal is coming from . . . is a paragon of other-worldliness who might have been a saint in old Russia but can only be looked upon benignly as a sort of fool in present-day America." [22]

Here is suggested one problem of the instructor that may cause considerable annoyance. As a member of a professional class, the young man and his wife and children must attempt to live up to

---

* "The systems underlying the cuts showed wide variation, but conformed to a pattern that tended to favor older staff members and the upper ranks. The young men and the lower ranks bore a double burden since the contractions in staff size localized in them." *Depression, Recovery and Higher Education,* op. cit., p. 49.

standards which are beyond their means. These standards are set by members of the faculty more able to meet them but the young man and his wife by virtue of their intimate association with these more fortunate members of the faculty feel compelled to spend money for children's schooling, cultural and recreational activities, housing, etc. in a manner that must be called lavish, in view of their income. This necessity of keeping up appearances creates irritation among the young in every profession and certainly the young professor is no exception. His uniqueness grows out of the meagerness of his income, and the comparatively greater intimacy of association in the academic profession.

What Is the Significance of These Facts?

We have thus far dealt with material of a statistical nature showing the financial condition of the profession. The important task of interpreting what these figures mean to the professor, his family, his students, the profession, and society in general now confronts us.

We can do no better than refer again to the thorough-going treatment of the subject presented by President Harper. It is not enough that the salary should cover only the cost of subsistence; to do effective work, he must spend a large proportion of his income in maintaining and adding to his mental and material equipment. He must spend considerable for books, for one thing.

"But learning is not all book-learning. In order that the professor shall be able to meet the expectations of the community he serves and still more, in order to do his work as a teacher as that work ought to be done, he must bring to his efforts the knowledge that comes . . . only at the cost of frequent and relatively extensive travel . . . in most cases his work suffers if he does not (travel). . . . He must also be enabled to contribute from his time and earnings to the organization and maintenance of learned societies as well as to profit by personal attendance at their meetings." [23]

Vacations, he goes on to emphasize, are not holidays; they are a part of the year's work. If part of this time must be spent in recuperation, this only bespeaks the need for a more generous salary and schedule of teaching. Under the best conditions the "vacation" is a fruitful period for the professor. Moreover, the business of "professing" requires the maintenance of a social standing. Usage has made it incumbent on him to identify himself with the best associations of the place in which he lives. There are the "customary pecuniary burdens incident to respectability." The community sets the standards in this regard and, if he wishes to retain respectability—and he does—he must pay the costs. "The necessity vitiates any crude comparisons between college salaries and the incomes of men exposed to no such social exactions."

What of his family? According to a professor writing in 1905, his family may suffer more than he does, for he may be devoted to scholarship in a spirit of renunciation.

"He is not supposed to be aware, even, that his food is plain, his shelter humble, his life monotonous. . . . But real self-effacement, silent deprivation, painful economy, are the lot of his wife." [24]

In 1938 the same idea is voiced by one who tells of the "Plight of the Professor's Wife." [25] Similarly, the *Nation* reports the assertion of a group of faculty wives, that "the only economy which in time enables us to live on our salaries is for us to have no babies." They describe a life in which economy is carried to the point of drabness and ill-health.[26] *

Important as this phase of the problem is, there are others to be considered. The community and the professor both suffer if the latter seeks to live to himself because of adverse economic circumstances.

"If the professor lives a life apart in order that he may be thrown neither with his economic equals who are culturally and educationally his inferiors, nor with his educational equals who set a financial pace he cannot follow, he must forfeit the place in the community which every self-respecting citizen desires. He must forfeit influence and condemn himself to a narrow society." [27]

---

* President J. R. Angell, in the Foreword to the Yale study, says that plenty of competent men are willing to live on modest stipends but "they rightly hesitate to subject their wives to the prospect of hard and unremitting physical drudgery, and their children to the limitations of the underprivileged in a time of general financial prosperity." *Incomes and Living Costs of a University Faculty*, Y. Henderson and M. Davie, Yale University Press, 1928, p. vii.

No doubt this writer, Professor Canby, has put his finger upon one important reason for the isolation of the professor. He is forced back upon himself by economic limitations and in the process he suffers, intellectually and emotionally, while the community is denied whatever advantages might accrue to his participation.

Scholarship and teaching are also penalized if salary is inadequate. No professor can give satisfactory service without peace of mind and few problems can disturb one's equanimity so quickly and so continuously as financial troubles. With regard to scholarship, the professor, even though possessing the ability for better things, is often compelled to spend his time and energies writing material that has a ready sale but makes no contribution to knowledge.

"Thus we have successive crops of more or less admirable school-books written by college professors. These books, if successful, yield large returns to the authors as well as the publishers, but they contain few, if any, real contributions to knowledge. Many college professors deliver addresses on all sorts of occasions, and for all amounts of money, by this means adding to their meager incomes at a sacrifice of time, of strength, and of the continuity of scholarly work which they and their colleges can ill afford." [28]

Nor can he carry on scholarly work without material aids such as books. Since his own income usually does not permit extensive purchases, he leans upon the library and the library fund. Yet here too there are obstructions. As one professor bitterly remarks,

"If he complains about the antediluvian library, the answer is, 'Why there's the Encyclopedia Britannica and the whole of the World's Best Literature. What more do you want, you snobs?' " [29]

Salary is an important factor in occupational selection and, in one form or another, more than a dozen periodicals refer to this point. It is said that low salary scales do not constitute sufficient pecuniary inducement to attract the best talent into the profession. At the beginning of the century an editor wrote,

"The community does not tempt the highest type of mind toward this calling because of the inadequacy of rewards . . ." [30]

Two years later the same magazine, *World's Work,* had more to say about the pay of teachers and what it denotes.

"The economic rule will hold that better pay would secure better teachers and better teachers would lift our educational work. We have not yet become really in earnest about educational work." [81]

Thus, if our educational work is to be lifted to a higher plane, we must pay much higher salaries so that the strongest men and women will enter the profession and become the real intellectual leaders of the nation. In spite of academic idealism the best men have something of worldly wisdom and will not "sacrifice a library, Europe, the education of their children, to the love of teaching." [82]

After the war, President Hadley of Yale wrote of low salaries as the great obstacle to good teaching. First-class men and women will not go into the profession especially in a time of conspicuously low rates of compensation. He did not think, however, that the unfortunate circumstance was due to an undervaluation of the work of the teacher by the community as a whole. Rather, it is due to an over-supply of those prepared to teach.

"The school and college authorities have been more concerned to make it easy to enter the profession of teaching than to make it worth while to stay there. They have kept up the supply of teachers by giving them their professional training at an almost nominal price. A young man who looks forward to the career of a college professor can get free tuition in almost any of our graduate schools if he has had a good college record and shows that he needs the money. . . . The market has been over-supplied with men who have no special qualifications for meeting its actual demands." [33]

President Lowell of Harvard mentioned the undesirable selective influence of low compensation, for this (1919) was a period of real economic distress in the profession and all hands of the pedagogical ship were being called on deck to decry the alarming condition of those charged with the responsibility of educating American youth.[34] The president of Princeton raised the provocative question, Are cheap teachers going to be good for your children? In the course of answering the query in the negative, he too records the counterselective trend.

"Even the most devoted educator must live. His normal desire for a family seems hardly unreasonable. If schools and colleges do not pay living wages, we can hardly blame the teachers for going elsewhere. Yet many a man, driven by the prospect of poverty into business, would be infinitely more valuable back in his college laboratory, carrying on research and imparting his wisdom and experience to students." [35]

Verification for this statement regarding an exodus from the profession comes from the *Literary Digest* which, in 1921, quotes Trevor Arnett as saying:

"Many teachers have left to enter far more lucrative fields. The mortality in college faculties in some cases is as high as eighty-five percent." [36]

Thus, low salaries not only keep the young of the best potentialities from entering the profession but, in times of unusually great economic stress, many of the more capable professors leave the universities.

Lest it may be thought that these are the extravagant utterances of educators during periods of high living costs, it may be worth while to show that the same principle is enunciated by recent writers. In 1935 the *Forum* carried an article on the subject which mentioned the counterselective tendency. It states that a survey conducted by one of our research councils found that the outstanding students were heading into other fields and not into the graduate schools for further training preliminary to teaching. The reasons given were mainly financial.

"Teaching . . . has not only no financial present but no financial future. We have made it a sort of madcap's prank for the young man of outstanding ability to go into the teaching profession. We are keeping the field consistently open chiefly for the person who is slightly lacking in stamina, energy, vision, and red blood and letting young people with splendid minds and a natural passion for the arts and sciences be reluctantly steered away into business and other professions out of sheer common sense." [37]

Frank Bohn makes a plea for $30,000 to $50,000 professorships. He believes that the starvation of the profession is a fundamental error in America and that, on the contrary, the first-class professors should receive as much income as the average corporation lawyer.

"If the whole field of American education offered five hundred positions with such salaries, the standing of the entire profession would be quickly elevated in the public mind." [38]

On the other hand, a number fear the intrusion of a commercial spirit into the profession.

"Large salaries commensurate with what equal ability would bring in other lines of work might be just, but would be undesirable, as they would tend to serve as bait to attract mercenary and lower types of men." [39]

The editors of *Forum* reported that there were scores of letters in 1925 protesting the position of Mr. Bohn in his article, "Fifty Thousand Dollars for Professors." They published one by Joseph Jastrow in the course of which he decries the proposed intrusion of Mammon: "The fallacy of the glorified salary is glaring in that it makes an idol of the financial criterion which is foreign to every proper spirit and conduct of the academic venture." In 1930 the editor of the *Nation* objected to a suggestion for high salaries that came from the new president of the University of Chicago in his inaugural address. Hutchins had said that "The only method by which we can attain our goal is to pay salaries that will enable the universities to compete with the business world for the best men." After reassuring its readers that it did not consider the existing scales adequate in general, the periodical reiterates the argument against very high salaries.

"Boost the professors as a group into the high salaried class . . . and you do two things. First, you multiply further . . . the number of hustling business men in our faculties. Second, and vastly more important, you create a strongly intrenched university vested interest in the status quo. . . . Rich professors are all too often social bourbons." [40]

Other contributors in other magazines repeat with minor variations the identical theme. One hopes that colleges will not succumb to the commercialism of the age. Higher salaries do not constitute the best means of attracting talent, for "the real scholar is just the one who is not attracted by large salaries." The college really needs the man who places scholarship above salary. [41] The *New Republic,* always sympathetic to professorial problems, echoes this sentiment.

"If education means anything at all . . . it leads a man out from the naive point of view in which the pecuniary criterion of value covers the universe like a blanket into a state of mind in which values are a little broader." [42]

The Professor Is Well Paid

On the other hand, there are those who do not find the salaries so lamentable. Ten years ago an editor wrote that the college teacher should not be pitied too readily, for his lot is a happy one. He teaches only about thirty-six weeks out of fifty-two, thus having opportunities for outside work. He has security—even the incompetent ones.

"He lives in a college town where his five to eight thousand a year, particularly when a dwelling house at nominal rent goes with the position, is reasonably ample. If he is a young instructor or assistant professor his salary may be but half as great; but, with some managing, it will usually meet modest bachelor requirements." [48]

Disregarding the attitude expressed toward the professor's lot as a whole, the author wonder where the editor got his information about salaries. If we speak in terms of averages, "five to eight thousand a year" is fantastic.* Moreoever, how many dwellings with nominal rents go with professorial appointments? Finally, the editor wishes to keep professors in a wifeless condition until they attain a rank above the assistant professorship! Who can stem the academic wrath at this juncture? However, members of the academic guild have expressed the same attitude toward the problem of salary. One autobiographical account (1917) tells of one who relishes the life which he is leading. He claims to be no self-pitying sort, although he wishes that his income were greater. Yet he feels that the scholar sacrifices income for freedom and security. The complaints of his colleagues about poverty have annoyed him for many years and he wonders, in all seriousness, whether these grumblers are really competent and energetic.

"When I read articles on the meanness of estate of the college professor, I am stimulated to a variety of speculation . . . are the unhappy indigents competent in their profession? Would their rewards in money or leisure be greater if they were in some other profession or in business? Are they

---

* Professor Harold Clark estimates that the average income per year for the college professor is $3050. This figure is based upon earnings for the period, 1920-36, and has a probable error of 10 percent.
   Harold F. Clark, *Life Earnings in Selected Occupations in the U. S.,* Harper and Brothers, 1937, page 5.

earning up to their reasonable capacity now, or are they spending the margins of their time and energy in the exhausting occupation of feeling abused?" [44]

Most of his associates are irritated at these views and some believe that he is talking only for effect. On the contrary, he seriously maintains that professors have the time and opportunities to earn supplementary income and, if they do not, they alone are to blame.

"Extras" are important items in many professorial budgets. A writer in the *American Magazine* (1920) tells that, in his college, "beyond a doubt eighty percent of the members of the faculty are having to supplement their incomes by outside work in order to keep body and soul together." [45] Another, calling himself a forager on Parnassus, gives public lectures and handles correspondence courses in order to pay his bills.

"Our professor began to forage in correspondence courses. He would get twenty-five dollars for a full course, so he made all his courses full. Each year he added a course. In four years he paid the doctor, the grocer, and the others. He didn't feel guilty because he was giving service." [46] *

There are others who scout the malcontents complaining that the world owes them a better living. One who has been teaching for thirty years asserts báldly that "there is at present (1929) not a more overpaid profession on earth than the academic." [47] Five years later another critic within the ranks voices sharply the same sentiment.

"As a matter of fact, the underpaid professor is more or less of a myth. Most professors get more than they deserve. They never actually teach more than fifteen hours a week, and that is exceptional. . . . A man who earns $3000 a year is not among the wealthy. But there are thousands of people who are working much harder and earning much less." [48]

He goes on to show how the same old courses are taught in the same old way year after year with the same notes and the same jokes. In refutation of the argument that preparation takes a lot

---

* "The studies of faculty income that have been made all show that supplementary earnings are important in the budget. . . . Miss Boothe found that eighty percent of the faculty members at institutions in her sample earned supplementary income." *Depression, Recovery and Higher Education*, op. cit. page 142.

of time, he defines class preparations as the process of hastily reading over old lecture notes. Talk about hours of preparation may sound very impressive to the unsophisticated but, so far as undergraduate courses are concerned, is just sheer nonsense.

PENSIONS

In the face of these somber facts is there no balm for his troubled mind? This is not the place to enter into a detailed analysis of the academic life but the factor of economic security may be mentioned. Security has soothed the anxiety in many a professorial breast. One of the important events affecting this security has been the establishment of a pension system sponsored by the Carnegie Foundation. Especially in the early years after Mr. Carnegie's gift the general magazines carried considerable discussion of the new pension plan. As *Collier's* reported the news in 1905,

"Mr. Carnegie, when he left for Europe, left a gift of $10,000,000 as a pension for incapacitated college professors of the United States, Canada, and Newfoundland. He said, 'I have reached the conclusion that the least rewarded of all professions is that of the teachers of our higher educational institutions.' " [49]

A few months later Mr. Henry S. Pritchett relays through the *Outlook* more information about the newly organized Carnegie Foundation for the Advancement of Teaching. He tells that, in Mr. Carnegie's letter of gift, he deplored the lack of financial support for the teacher and the effect which this lack has in discouraging men from the profession. Carnegie's purpose was to "establish the principle of the retiring salary in academic life in America as a means of advancing the cause of higher education."

"The purpose of the foundation is described in the following words: 'To provide retiring pensions without regard to race, sex, creed, or color, for the teachers of universities, colleges, and technical schools in the United States, the Dominion of Canada, and Newfoundland' . . . and 'in general, to do and perform all things necessary to encourage, uphold, and dignify the profession of the teacher and the cause of higher education.' " [50]

Yet immediately we find voices raised in protest against the plan as a solution for the financial plight of the college teacher.

A pension is looked upon as a poor substitute for adequate compensation during a man's active career. A promise of economic security after retirement cannot relieve distress in the present for those who have families to rear. However, for men approaching old age after years of low salaries a pension is the sole salvation.

"For younger men . . . Mr. Carnegie's pension system is not the only salvation, nor the one which the self-respecting and independent man would choose. If Mr. Carnegie had directed his generous gift and the weight of his influence against a scale of salaries which forces the college professor to celibacy or to want, there should be greater satisfaction in the feeling of gratitude and appreciation merited by such a gift. Let the salaries of college men be what they should . . . and there will be no occasion to fear an indigent old age." [51]

About the same time another periodical agrees that the simplest way to improve the economic position would be to raise salaries so that professors could save for old age out of their additional incomes. But whenever colleges obtain more funds they spend them for plant and equipment "in order to keep abreast of their competitors." Thus, under the circumstances, the pension represents the wisest move possible.[52] Professor Jastrow feels that there is little hope for the solution of the problems besetting American universities from within academic walls. An extraneous organization like the Foundation is needed, although it should enlarge its conception of the "advancement of teaching."

"It falls within the scope of the Carnegie Foundation to emphasize, by all possible channels of influence, the underlying objects of its existence; in this instance such emphasis may prevent the use of the retiring allowance as a compensation for the more sorely needed increase of active income." [53]

President Thwing of Western Reserve University agrees that trustees should not unload their duties of making proper compensation to the members of their faculties upon the Foundation. Salaries must still be improved in spite of the great steel man's generosity. He too mentions how ambitious young men of talent are more likely to be attracted to the academic life.[54] One professor in 1914, after the pension plan had been in operation for eight years, pessimistically asserts that the colleges, not the teachers, are the chief beneficiary, for they can pay lower salaries and they profit by the greater efficiency of teachers freed from financial anxieties concerning the future.[55]

Hardly had the plan begun to function before a revision was introduced. While pensions at the age of sixty-five were to be given as before, and indeed with some additional liberality, pensions based simply on twenty-five years' service as a professor were no longer to be granted except for serious disability.* The officials of the Foundation claimed that the service pension enabled the colleges to get rid of poor teachers and encouraged some teachers to become ultra-critical toward their institutions. The *Nation* comments,

"This revision of the rules opens up two questions of wholly distinct character—first, the ethical propriety of making such a change . . . and secondly, the desirability of the new rule as compared with the old, taken in itself. . . . On the purely fiscal side of the case . . . the long and short of the matter seems to be that a gross miscalculation was made." [56]

This writer goes on to state that the plans of many professors have no doubt been disturbed by this alteration. They expected the service pension and now it is abolished at a stroke, without consultation with those affected and without warning. Yet amid the welter of adverse sentiment there is one correspondent in the same magazine who points out the financial problem faced by the Foundation, the simple fact being that it has been found too expensive to carry out the original intention.

Mr. Carnegie had stipulated that colleges and universities connected with various denominations should not be covered by the pension plan. In 1914 the *Independent* reported an attack made by Thomas W. Churchill, President of the New York Board of Education, on the Foundation. Mr. Churchill charged that the Foundation had virtually bribed denominational colleges to change their charters, since many had found it expedient to sever official connection with the church in order to qualify for the pensions. The *Independent*, however, denies Carnegie's hostility to religion.[57]

---

* A service pension differs from a retirement pension in that the former is based upon years of service, irrespective of age, while the latter is based on age.

Mr. Clyde Furst, secretary of the Foundation, issued a statement that was reported in the *Literary Digest* in which he explained the reasons for the stipulation.

> "The only reason for the provision . . . that retiring pensions shall be paid only to teachers in institutions not under the control of a sect, nor imposing any theological test as a condition of connection therewith, is administrative efficiency. If a college were owned or controlled by another organization it would be very difficult . . . to deal with that college alone. A foundation like this cannot, for instance, deal with a national organization like the Catholic Church." [58]

In 1915, after ten years of operation, Mr. Pritchett, President of the Foundation, reviews the whole problem in the *Independent*. Up to this time the pension has been free, that is, the entire financial burden has been carried by the Foundation. Now the advisability of a continuance of the free pension is questioned and it is cautiously suggested that a contributory system may be more desirable.[59] This is not the first time that allusion is made to the charitable nature of the whole plan. Nine years before the *Saturday Evening Post* had raised the point that, coming from a private source, the pension would savor of charity.

> "As long as Mr. Carnegie lives and for a good while after, the Carnegie pension will savor of charity, no matter how impersonally it may be administered. If the pension came directly from the institution that the professor had served all his life, there would be less charity to it; it might be considered a legitimate part of the pay for faithfulfully performed work." [60]

A year later (1907) Dr. Thwing, secretary of the Foundation, had emphasized that the "retiring allowance is not a largess, not a favor . . . it is an attempt to give proper compensation to the college teacher . . . a deferred payment on salary account."[61]

Finally in 1918 Mr. Pritchett writes a detailed justification of the change from the free pension to the contributory. This change is probably deemed advisable in view of the threatened depletion of the original ten million dollars.* The whole problem is said to

---

* Dr. David Starr Jordan, a member of the board of the Foundation, denied that the reason for the change was financial.[62]

resolve itself into three practical questions. First, is the free pension system in the interest of the college teacher? Second, if a free pension is not in their interest, what are the fundamental principles upon which a system must rest in order to be socially just and economically secure? Third, if the system shall be altered, what is a fair fulfillment of the expectations of teachers who have been affiliated under the old non-contributory allowances? He then goes on to demonstrate that continuation of the existing system is not in the interest of the professor. In the long run salaries will adjust themselves to the assumed benefits of such a pension. As a result, the pay of the whole group is depressed although only a minority will receive grants in old age—"for in all pension systems only a minority come to pensionable age." Thus, through preventing proper increases in salary, the free pension works a practical injustice. Moreover, there is the ever-growing cost of such a plan, the implication probably being that, with increased pensioners, the grants would diminish to microscopic proportions.[63]

Next, he takes up the second question, fundamental principles. A commission composed of college teachers, presidents, and trustees and officers of the Foundation finally evolved the following four principles:

"1.—The function of a pension system is to secure the individual against the risk of dependence due to old age or disability . . .

2.—The obligation to secure this protection rests first upon the individual . . .

3.—The obligation of the employer to cooperate in sustaining a pension system is primarily a financial one and in the second place a moral one.

4.—A pension system . . . should rest upon the cooperation of employee and employer."

The upshot of the whole situation was that an agency called the "Teachers' Insurance and Annuity Association of America" was established with a capital of one million dollars supplied by the Carnegie Corporation. In accordance with this set-up, college teachers may purchase insurance and old-age annuities by paying one-half the premium, the respective institutions employing the services of the professors to contribute the other half. Meanwhile, it is decided that the Foundation will continue payment on a non-contributory basis to six thousand teachers already connected with it. Part of this justification of the new plan is repeated a year later, also in the *Atlantic Monthly,* upon the death of Mr. Carnegie. Again Pritchett insists that a free pension is not the solution for teachers in a democracy.[64] *

It is not hard to imagine that many received this official pronouncement with fear and anger. In spite of the tact evident in the aforementioned articles by the president of the Foundation, many professors saw chiefly the simple fact that they would be compelled to dig down into their own pockets for that which they had expected to receive *gratis* on account of the Carnegie philanthropy. Jastrow describes several criticisms:

> "When recently the Foundation proposed to substitute for the several substitutes of the original fine intention a scheme of insurance by which the Foundation offered to collect from the impecunious professors . . . whose characters it has been subtly abusing, the scheme was not enthusiastically received. . . . No one reading the replies can fail to be struck by the profound distrust and bitter rèsentment that have been aroused among members of the academic profession . . ."[65]

Even in its original intention, it is pointed out further, the Carnegie Foundation for the Advancement of Teaching had no thought of stimulating the professorial guild to genuine self-assertion. It was to provide substantial retiring allowances for a limited number of worthy institutions—and now even this purpose is being amended. Later in the same year the same writer blasts away at a "complacent Foundation." Ironically, he calls attention to the fact that only recently has Mr. Pritchett "providentially" discovered a new social philosophy which held that a free pension was demoralizing. To him there is one great benefit resultant from the management of the Foundation: it has aroused such

---

* The argument is advanced that the free pension is demoralizing to the individual. This point carries considerable weight in an individualistic culture which values individual initiative and self-reliance. A contributory system represents a compromise between faith in individual initiative and the attitude that the employer or society at large must be held responsible for the employee's welfare after retirement.

widespread opposition among professors as to awaken a desirable class consciousness and a "realization of the seriousness of the Foundation's menace to their interests when it is in alien and unsympathetic hands." Who constitute these alien and unsympathetic hands? A board of directors composed of men selected from university administrations.

"Thus securely entrenched as a self-perpetuating board of university presidents, a board on which no member of the profession for whose benefit the pension exists has been able to gain representation, the trustees were free to interpret the conventional clause reserving the right to make such changes as circumstances might indicate, as giving them a free hand for repudiating obligations and posing necessities as virtues." [66] *

Except for a critical article on the Foundation, published in the *Nation* in 1929, nothing seems to have been written on the subject of pensions after 1919.

EXPLANATION OF THE ECONOMIC CONDITION OF THE PROFESSION

We come now to the problem of interpreting the foregoing material. With a few exceptions salaries are deemed inadequate by the magazines. Without accepting the attitudes expressed in the foregoing pages as necessarily valid, we are concerned at this point in accounting for the economic condition of the profession.

There are those who see in the economic situation an objective index of the attitude toward learning found in America. Such an interpretation is easy to suggest but difficult to establish scientifically. The attitude toward learning probably varies according to a number of circumstances, such as class status, size and location of the community, and the definition of "learning." The probability of ambivalence in the attitude toward learning further complicates the problem. While it is not unreasonable to assume that a greater respect for the things of the mind would be reflected in professorial salaries, one cannot draw hasty inferences concerning the correlation of salary with prestige.

---

* Cf. J. M. Cattell, *Carnegie Pensions,* Science Press, 1919.

The maintenance of academic dignity may be somewhat expensive. There are colleagues to be entertained, college functions to attend which require evening clothes, and entertainment of students and alumni during such occasions as founder's day and commencement. Such social demands upon the professor are probably greater than in the other professions which are also better paid (with the exception of the ministry). These social obligations may account for the fact that faculty members are "house-proud." According to Henderson and Davie, "the faculty are straining to live in better neighborhoods than they can well afford on their salaries. They impose this standard of living on themselves or are forced to adopt it because of the social pressure exerted by the community, which places them in a higher social category than their incomes warrant."* Apropos of this matter, Veblen states: "University men are conventionally required to live on a scale of expenditure comparable with that in vogue among the well-to-do businessmen, while their university incomes compare more nearly with the lower grades of clerks and salesmen."† In addition, as several writers have pointed out, no professor can evade altogether such obligations as the purchase of books, subscription to magazines, membership in learned societies, contributions to charity and to endowment drives launched by the local college. Expenditure for travel may really be counted as part of his professional expenses, for the person of intellectual tastes cannot afford to become or remain provincial. All of these items indicate the demands upon the professor's salary.

Professor Yandell Henderson, chairman of the committee on the academic standard of living which studied incomes and living costs of the Yale faculty, has called attention to another consideration that he thinks is of great importance in accounting for the financial plight of the faculty. The trouble is that there are too many teachers on college faculties. Other professions such as the medical are taking greater precautions than ever before in limiting the numbers of practitioners but the professor very often

---

* Op. cit. page 67.
† *The Higher Learning in America,* Huebsch, 1918, page 161.

fails to see where his own economic interest lies and talks of the desirability of small classes and large instructional staffs. Henderson, being much concerned about the intellectual quality of college faculties and asserting that this end can only be accomplished through more adequate salary schedules, is quite emphatic about his proposed remedy.

"The possibilities of higher salaries, so far as the faculty can influence it, depends wholly on covering a larger number of students hours per week with fewer, or at least without more, teachers. It is therefore strongly in the financial interest of the faculty as a whole to decrease the small-class type of teacher, except when he shows distinct scholarly ability, and to encourage every teacher, without increasing his courses or his hours in the classroom, to teach as large classes as he can efficiently." *

Nor does he view with approbation the enlargement of the facilities of the university in the way of new schools, for these only increase the faculty and make sums set aside for raising the level of salaries less effective. This principle is well-known to economists who have much to say on the subject of the relation of value and scarcity† but faculty members in many colleges seem to overlook it time and time again in their analyses of professional problems. Instead, they prate of reduction of class sizes and the prestige of belonging to expanding departments and expanding universities—at least the unwise do. American labor has long recognized how European immigration constitutes a threat to its economic life and the country has put into operation quota laws of increasing restriction. College professors might take a tip from the laboring man and work to introduce immigration restrictions on the campus. One effective method of attacking this problem would involve rigid selection in the graduate school, so that fewer and better Ph. D.'s would emerge. It would very likely be one of the most salutary influences possible. Higher education would be advanced notably in this country if candidates for teaching positions were carefully sieved all along the line of their embryonic

---

* Bulletin of the A.A.U.P., Vol. 15, No. 7, Nov., 1929, page 532.

† Cf. T. N. Carver's "Cure for Poverty" in his *Essays in Social Justice,* Chap. 14, Harvard Press, 1915.

development. We would have fewer teachers but these would be more adequately paid for their professional services.†

The American Association of University Professors has as one of its purposes the improvement of the economic condition of the profession, although it is difficult to ascertain its general influence in this regard. It is true, however, that various local chapters have been able to accomplish economic reforms.* In 1906 the *Nation* editorialized on this subject.

> "The bitter cry of the ill-paid college professor is filling the land. . . . From the point of view of organized labor, the cause of the trouble is as clear as the remedy is simple. College professors have no unions. They neither keep down the number of apprentices nor shut out 'scab' competitors. . . . While the Erie Railroad employees are vigorously demanding more pay, and threatening to tie up the road, the non-unionized professors are being driven to such desperate [sic] expedients as marrying rich wives." [67]

While the very suggestion of "unionization" has been vulgar to many, certainly it cannot be denied that, since 1915, the A.A.U.P. has endeavored to secure for its members many of the same advantages that the trade unions have striven for. Terminology is not important. Yet, due in part to the individualism bred by intellectual activity and in part to the desire to preserve dignity, the academic man has been slow to realize the possibilities of progress through collective action. "Not dollars but decorum" seems to be the slogan of many. As a matter of fact, it is by no means certain that collective action degrades the profession. Even college executives have at times spoken in favor of such action. In 1920, when the financial plight of the professor was especially dire, the acting president of Bryn Mawr college wrote as follows:

---

† It has been suggested that the number of unemployed Ph. D's. could be reduced if more of them went into our secondary schools.

Cf. "The Doctorate and the Depression," R. G. Harris *School and Society,* Vol. 36, page 498.

"Too Many Ph. D's.?" E. Faris *American Journal of Sociology,* Vol. 39, page 509.

* The author is well acquainted with one university where the local chapter of the American Association of University Professors has made definite strides toward better salaries.

"I wish professors would unite and strike for better salaries. It would be less of a disaster for the country to have the teachers unite and demand higher salaries than it is to have the present salaries continue. In the latter case, professors will strike, not in unison, but individually, and every ambitious and intelligent man and woman will withdraw from the teaching profession." [68]

There are other reasons for the salary situation. Veblen was not the first to call attention to the manner in which money is spent for material equipment.

"The evidence is irresistible that the time has come when our college benefactors can perform the greatest service, not by devoting their money to buildings and material equipment, but to strengthening the teaching force." [69]

A grade teacher who later secures a position in a university testifies to the same end:

"In the university I found much the same injustice to teachers that prevailed all down the line. The legislature of the state at each session voted a million dollars to the support of the university, but it did not go toward teachers' salaries. It went into buildings, into landscape gardening, into paying the coach so that the university might have a winning football team." [70]

That this same comment is made today is indicated by a recent article in *Forum*.

"The physical equipment of our great institutions is impressive but a veil is drawn over the circumstances under which 'Mark Hopkins' actually lives when he is not sitting on the other end of his rather gorgeous twentieth-century 'log'." [71]

Yet the fact is that the fruits of the educational process are not easily measured. There is an intangibility about education which defies statistical treatment and makes it difficult to dramatize the work of the teacher. On the other hand, the physical equipment may be readily perceived and has greater publicity value with the general public.

". . . the professor's qualifications have never been standardized, nor the amount and kind of duties to be expected of him. . . . Benefactors are willing to put their money in new buildings and physical equipment because they are sure of getting their money's worth in something that can be seen and measured in terms of common exchange. . . . Even universities themselves prefer to divert an endowment from its own avowed purpose of raising the payroll and to establish new departments instead. The latter show off nicely in the catalogue . . . but a raise in salary looks like so much money sunk without visible return." [72]

In view of what has been said concerning the economic condition of the profession, it may be suggested that whatever monasticism prevails represents a more or less satisfactory adjustment to the financial situation. Denied large material rewards, the professor may develop an ideology which emphasizes the primacy of non-material values, especially the intellectual. Perhaps this factor helps to explain the reported tendency of college professors to mix rather exclusively with their own professional kind. In this sense the academic profession resembles a religious cult living apart because its values are not appreciated by society at large. Finding itself at odds with the values of a commercial culture, the members of the profession find consolation in contemplating its own values and calling to mind the great names which have carried its traditions through the years. Indeed, many of the profession are inclined to frown upon the colleague who is commercial-minded (at an earlier time the latter would have been called worldly). Finally, if his unimpressive income impels an adherence to monastic ideals, he is only illustrating the mechanism of rationalization which is common to all manner of men everywhere.*

II. Academic Life

Income, though quite important, does not tell the whole story. Common sense tells us that there are many conditions of work which must be figured in along with salary or wages in arriving at an estimate of the possible satisfactions and dissatisfactions of the job. In analyzing the academic life there are two phases that will be omitted for the present, the problem of teaching and the relation

---

* It is pertinent, in view of the numerous complaints concerning salary, to point out that professors are not unique in this respect. Professor Clark has said: "One of the most striking things revealed by the investigation was the consistency with which each occupation maintained it was underpaid." *Life Earnings,* op. cit. p. 15.

of the faculty to the administration, for these will be treated separately in subsequent chapters.

Perhaps the most frequently mentioned advantage of the professor's life is the leisure that he possesses. His hours in the classroom are comparatively few and the vacations are long.

"As a general rule, professors hold classes only thirty-six weeks out of the fifty-two. These thirty-six weeks are often five-day weeks, and the number of hours spent in classrooms and lecture halls frequently does not exceed twelve or fourteen." [1]

Another writer speaks about the luxuries of being a professor, one of which is the luxury of "wallowing in time and in long vacations." [2] But this same person hastens to add that these luxuries must be paid for in salary and autonomy. A third pays his respects to the vacation but reminds those inclined to consider the profession a "snap" that the work is strenuous while it lasts.

"Here and there a teacher frankly admits that he teaches chiefly for the vacations; and it would be affectation for any of us to pretend that we do not like holidays, even though they may be one cause why, during the rest of the year, we work all hours of day and night, and seldom have time for the business man's slender solace of thinking how tired he is." [3]

All of this means that the professor has a great deal of freedom. He is free in not being tied down to his work for eight hours every day. As the writer above suggests, this freedom is not without its price but there are no doubt many academic persons like the following one who do not feel that the price is too high.

"Here is my own case, for example—eight hours a week of class during about thirty-three weeks in the year. That is my fixed schedule. I put in at least fifty hours more each week in reading and writing. . . . For three whole days out of seven I am absolutely foot-loose and, although there are not many days when I do not know the feeling of honest fatigue, my fatigue is my own choice, and in one hundred and sixty hours of the week I know I am free to loaf or to work at option." [4]

At this juncture one of the unfavorable characterizations of the professor may be recalled: he was accused of being lazy by several (academic) writers. In view of the easy hours of the teaching

schedule, it is not surprising that such a criticism should be made.*
It is not in accord with the present purpose, however, to call the
professor by unpleasant names; rather, the desire is to understand
the problems of the profession. One reason for the leisure is that
intellectuals find it an indispensable condition of their work.

"Yet the truth is that six or eight hours a week of first-rate class work,
informed as to the latest results of research, thoroughly digested and carefully presented, will keep a professor busy. If he attempts more, he de-
generates into a machine. . . . The time spent in experimentation that is
not immediately productive, in reading, in mulling over his ideas while he
walks . . . is not pure loafing or genteel recreation. This is the very process
by which he subjugates his facts, assimilates his learning, and repairs his
scholarship." [6]

In a similar vein, a professor's wife rises to her husband's defense
and upbraids those faculty wives who feel free to use up their
husbands' time in household chores. He must, she urges, spend
many hours reading and discussing the problems of his field if he is
to secure mastery over his subject. She blames wives for some of
the intellectual smallness of college teachers.

"Perhaps we wives, fully as much as meager salaries, are to blame for the
intellectual smallness of our college teachers and for the loss to the world
of poets whose wings have been clipped in the basement laundry." [7]

As a matter of fact, there are other considerations that modify
the amount of the leisure. Having evolved beyond the days of a
predominantly agricultural nation, we no longer live in an era of
winter schooling and summer farming. Summer schools are legion,
where for six to twelve weeks the work of the college goes on
unabated. Moreover, aside from the time consumed in "repairing
his scholarship," the professor finds other activities making inroads
on his time. An editorial writer in the *Saturday Evening Post*
shows considerable insight into this problem.

---

* "There is the amusing yarn about the hick legislator who was appointed
on a committee to investigate conditions at a certain state university. 'And
just how much do you teach, sir?' he demanded sharply of one of the professors who had been summoned before the committee. 'Ten hours' replied
the nervous pedagogue. 'That sounds like a good day's work to me, gentlemen,' observed the legislator, excusing the witness." [5]

"Many demands upon the professor's time are omitted from this lean schedule. He must mark papers, hold conferences with students, conduct seminars and journal clubs, sit on sundry faculty committees, prepare papers for learned societies and their publications, and accumulate notes and references for the books he is presumably writing." [8]

In this connection it is pertinent to quote the remark of one professor who, when asked how he felt about academic freedom, replied that "all the academic freedom he wanted was freedom from committee meetings and a chance to go on with his work." [9] Evidently, this man would have acquiesced readily to Laski's characterization of academic committees as "soul-destroying." Probably few outside the confines of the university realize the enormous time and energy expended by a substantial number of faculty members in the work of the innumerable committees.

The leisure of the profession takes on added attractiveness when the next advantage is juxtaposed, for what more pleasant way to spend some of this time than in discourse with congenial associates? Forty years ago Professor Bliss Perry, discussing the life of a college professor, wrote:

"Your life-long associates will be gentlemen. . . . There is nothing more pleasing than the association of a professor with his colleagues and nothing more delightful than their twilight conversations." [10]

Others corroborate this view. One professor, comparing teaching and business, states that the average professor is more happily situated than the average business man. One reason for this is that "associates devoted to intellectual pursuits make very pleasant companions in such time as they can give to each other." [11] The congenial social relations are not confined to academic colleagues, however. Several refer to the opportunity for greater association with one's family. A professor's wife describes how her husband has a leisurely breakfast, gets to school by nine, and is usually back by noon for lunch and a chat. There is usually a colleague in to tea or supper or to spend the evening.

"A student may drop in, some young instructors. The numbers swell. Tongues fly, arguments grow heated. The repast is elastic, even on a professor's salary." [12]

Not all of the congeniality of his associations is found with colleagues. The contacts with the students are mentioned frequently too. One writer speaks of the stimulation of being in contact with "the healthy optimism of youth." [13] Another tells how he is "kept in the constant companionship of youth, which is ever renewed stimulus and inspiration." [14] A third refers to the humor and pathos of youth.[15] Still another tells about an important discovery that he has made in this connection.

"It took several years for me to grasp the fact that, in so puzzling a world of men and affairs, my opportunity for the give and take of friendship lay in the members of my classes, and that perhaps they would let me know them, if I would let them know me." [16]

Nor do congenial colleagues and refreshing students complete the picture. The collegiate environment affords intellectual and artistic opportunities through lectures, concerts, and kindred entertainment. These make possible unlimited personal development in respect to information, ideas, and appreciation. Some, of course, are motivated, under such conditions, to become creative along intellectual and artistic lines. This phase of the professorial life need not be described at great length but its advantages constitute one of the major attractions of the profession for many.

"The professor's work has something of the charm of a hobby— a blending of vocation and avocation." [17] Certainly it may be said that for those who find in their academic work the aforementioned advantages the professional activities devolving upon them are far from onerous. It is doubtful whether we should use the term "work", for it smacks of that which is dull, routinized, and more or less unpleasant. For those who find the freedom and congeniality of the profession its dominating attributes, the "duties" of office partake, in reality, of the nature of a hobby. Their emotions flow into their academic tasks. Life is full of meaning and purpose; in a word, they have made an excellent adjustment to their environment. However, one suspects that there are few in any pursuit so well adjusted as this. Perhaps those writers who describe the charm of the academic life are incurably romantic, refusing to face the other side of the ledger; or even if they are telling the whole story as regards their own situation, generalization is still unwarranted.

Our analysis of the advantages is not yet complete, however. The professor has security. This feature of the profession has been especially to the front during the depression. As these writers indicate, many prefer the small but steady income to that which fluctuates considerably or is uncertain at best. Moreover, there is security in the fact that the struggle to maintain one's position is not so intense.

"Consider also the security which hedges the college professor. The stern but invigorating rule of the outside world, 'Produce or quit,' is not inscribed over academic portals. The tedious lecturer may have some of his courses turned over to a colleague, but he is let down easily and is allowed to retain his title and to receive his pay. Every large university, in deference to academic traditions, carries much dead wood of this sort." [16]

Several mention the Carnegie pension plan in connection with security. In spite of the criticisms launched against the Carnegie Foundation, it would be difficult to hold that it has not augmented the security of the profession. Very likely many academic families have echoed the sentiment of a widow who wrote a letter of gratitude to the Foundation, concluding with a thankful "God bless Andrew Carnegie."

The desire for security is one of the fundamental human wishes, according to W. I. Thomas. Especially during times of economic stress, this advantage is to the fore and many in commercial pursuits cast envious eyes at the professor. No doubt, too, a great many persons gravitate to the academic field in order to escape some of the hazards of existence. There must be many, fearful of the uncertainties of commercial competition, who select an academic career.

Prestige is another perquisite of the profession. An editorial writer states that "he has a gentle and dignified calling . . . and an esteemed position in his community." [19] A recent contributor (1938), who calls himself Professor Anonymous, emphasizes the same point.

"Lastly, he enjoys a certain gratifying prestige. Not so many years ago, the college professor . . . was a standard comic character in the eyes of the American people. That is no more. The Brain Trust . . . was the first public admission that the college professor might have something on the ball . . ." [20]

Prestige is part of the psychic income of the profession. While the "economic man" of the classical economist may be a convenient abstraction in studying economic processes, social psychology recognizes that human nature is a broader psychological whole. The wish for recognition may be satisfied in non-material ways.

All in all, if we may believe these accounts, the professorial life is very attractive. Professor Perry waxes enthusiastic over the "imaginative charm that invests the existence of the solitary scholar." [21] Henry S. Canby refers to the picturesque caricature of the professor in novels and the theater, according to which "he lives serene and untroubled among his books." [22] A third academician states that "the call of the lecture-hall and the laboratory is the call of happiness. . . . Our work is our passion." [23] There is no reason to doubt that the academic life holds all these advantages for many professors, although due allowance must be made for an idealistic bias that creeps into the thinking of many as soon as they set themselves to composing a popular article.

Yet it cannot be stressed too much that here we have the easy generalizations of the common-sense method of analysis. Therefore, it is to be expected that contradictory statements should appear in the periodicals. What are the stated drawbacks of the profession? Let us survey the more somber colors in the academic pattern.

The professor is said to lead a cloistered existence. About forty years ago one magazine carried a quotation from Longfellow on this point.

"What a strange picture the university presents to the imagination! The lives of scholars in their cloistered stillness—professors who study fifteen hours a day, and never see the world but on a Sunday." [24]

A doctor of philosophy who forsook academic groves for the marts of trade speaks of the manner in which his colleagues withdrew into "the comparative quiet and detachment of the university quadrangle." [25] As early as 1897, one professor asserts that the academic man is more cloistered than formerly.

"There was a time when the college professor was respected and revered by the townspeople. His word carried weight in any political meeting . . . (He) is criticized now for not mixing in town life. He takes no interest in important current questions." [26] *

This aspect of the academic life can hardly be questioned. Living amid an environment of books and youth, the professor is usually (though there are some exceptions) removed from the practical affairs of economic and political life. This appears true in spite of the trend toward a more practical type reported by many.†

Those describing academic life in glowing terms have had something to say concerning the congenial colleagues that the campus affords. Others, on the contrary, find them narrow specialists who do not speak a common language.

"In no American college today . . . can a faculty be found in which all the members are bound together by any single important connecting link of past scholarly acquirement or current intellectual interest. . . . The result of all this is that the members of college faculties are deprived of one of the most valuable sources of mental stimulation, the mutual exchange of ideas on matters of common knowledge and serious intellectual bearing." [27]

Specialists, as such, may not be very congenial companions. In the primary-group relations, interaction is personal rather than specialized and impersonal. Such relations call for a wholeness of personality not characteristic of the specialist as such. Thus, specialized individuals may experience difficulties in social intercourse with each other on account of attitudinal barriers.‡

---

* It is perhaps typical of the thinking of a great many periodical writers that this same writer five years later publishes an article showing that professors are more practical and closer to their fellow citizens than formerly. One may legitimately doubt whether such a transformation has come about between 1897 and 1902.

† "That is the reason why our universities have so little influence on American life. You are theorists, immuned in your cloisters, lulled to sleep by chimes. . . . You are competing with yourselves in a secluded corner of the universe. Get out!" Robert Herrick, *Chimes,* Macmillan, 1926, p. 181.

‡ Henry Adams remarked that in his day Cambridge Society was a faculty-meeting without business.

Nor do all agree that the contacts with the students are stimulating and inspiring. One professor, urging a young instructor to abandon his academic career, reminds him that in his formative years as a teacher his contact will be only with the immature.[28] While college teachers may take pleasure in the company of youth and may even, occasionally, be stimulated intellectually, this latter relation of mutual intellectual stimulation is likely to be exceptional. Though adolescents cannot be blamed for their immaturity, nonetheless it presents a problem that has baffled men besides Henry Adams. The inability of the young to marshall formidable rebuttals to the teacher's interpretations because of their immaturity and because of their institutionalized subordination helps to account for the dogmatic manner that infects many a professor.

"The inevitable tendency in teaching is to lay down the law to youths who either cannot or do not care to contradict. The professor is an authority and the older he gets the more authoritative he becomes. . . . In the industrial world men are always putting their ideas against those of their equals, as well as of their inferiors and superiors." [29]

The drudgery and routine of the profession are pointed out by several critics. G. Stanley Hall, connected with educational work as teacher and administrator throughout his lifetime, has admitted that "lapse to mechanism and routine is the iron law of all educational systems and is as universal as gravity."[30] A professor, now in the business world, looks back upon his academic days and makes comparisons.

"As an instructor my days had been full of the drudgery of correcting papers and painfully preparing lectures. I had very little time left for the original and creative work upon which the instructor's future almost depends. Now, however, my hack work is done by a stenographer or by subordinate clerks. If instructorships and assistant professorships were equipped with a dictaphone and a stenographer, what a difference there would be in the attractiveness of these positions." [31]

There is a popular notion to the effect that the teacher "gets in a rut." The monotony involved in repeating the same material year after year probably alienates many a young person from teaching.* On the other hand, every profession has its share of routine tasks.

"Of course they have papers to correct while they are in the lower ranks, and paper-correcting is fatiguing. But it is no more fatiguing than what every lawyer or physician or business man has to do." [32]

A number challenge the idea that the professor enjoys a high degree of prestige. Some of the unfavorable remarks refer to the attitude of the public in general while others concern some particular group, chiefly business men. It is true that several magazines refer to the enhancement of the social standing of the profession since the advent of the New Deal although here again opinion is divided. One academic writer, for example, asserts that

"The recent use which President Roosevelt has made of certain professors has done more to redeem the credit of the American college than anything that has happened in a long time. Those young economists and others like them in the country who have been called to solve actual problems will be the kind of teacher youth will turn to when they go back to their classes." [33]

But it is not difficult to discover a contrary opinion on this very matter. Another professor sees a diminution in prestige during the last few years.

"The professor is no longer respected by the newspapers. . . . Judged by this most infallible register of public attitudes the professor's popularity is on the wane." [34] †

Previous to the rise of the brain trusters plenty of adverse comments on prestige may be found. Some describe the attitude of business men as one of contempt. Others venture to record a trend toward lower status over a period of years. In 1902 Professor Ladd wrote as follows:

---

* "The wistful remark of a high-school teacher, 'I just wasn't brought up to do anything interesting. So I'm teaching.' possibly represents the situation with many." *Middletown,* op. cit., p. 207.

† Not much over a year after this article appeared, the country was treated to a striking refutation of the statement that the newspapers are an "infallible register of the public attitudes." In November, 1936, it was estimated that eighty percent of the newspaper circulation of the country had supported the Republican candidate in the national election.

"It would no doubt be difficult to demonstrate that the teaching body . . . is less highly regarded in comparison with other university interests than it was in former times. I believe this, however, to be true." [35]

A dozen years later a similar statement was made by another professor.

"Each decade has seen the quondam idol shrinking and slipping, until today he is full low and none so poor to do him reverence." [36]

Thus, here again we must record the inevitable inconsistencies of generalizations based on fragmentary observation and experience. Then too in dealing with elusive phenomena such as prestige the temptation is always present, particularly with those writers unacquainted with the discipline of scientific thought, to project onto an imaginary "public" one's own feelings. Nevertheless, enough has been said to indicate that all are not of one mind in regard to prestige.

The aforementioned "Professor Anonymous" details a number of aspects of the academic life which he considers to be disadvantages.

"You will be assigned to committees to study and report on matters which are incapable of solution. . . . You'll be drawn into finespun discussions that have no more connection with reality than has Surrealism. . . . You'll be surrounded by ponderous minds which give forth commonplace observations in deep and solemn tones." [37]

Nevertheless he admits that such matters are no worse than sales meetings or a typical board conference.

Some of the most important and interesting aspects of the academic life are neglected by the general magazines. There is very little to be found concerning faculty relations and politics, a subject which represents an exciting chapter and one largely unexplored.* Some material was found in regard to faculty meetings, however, most of it being adversely critical. John Erskine,

---

* For vivid descriptions of academic life the reader is referred to the general bibliography. Besides several novels listed there the author recommends Canby's *"Alma Mater"* Chap. 6 and, for the minutiae of academic life, the recent collection of humorous sketches by James Parker entitled, *Academic Procession*.

writing in *Liberty* a few years ago, asserted that "the faculty, taken as individuals, are as fine a lot of men as you'll find in any profession, but put them together in a faculty meeting and they promptly go mad."[38] Another thinks it strange that men, who presumably have been subjected to intellectual discipline, should rattle on aimlessly in meetings. He offers the following disjointed account of the phrases habitually found there.

" 'On the other hand, I very often feel——in thinking the matter over though I can see——It has been my experience, however——Well of course, I shall have to concede that——' The delicate balancing of one side against another. That delicious teetering moment before it becomes apparent that both sides (in the last analysis) are right." [39]

Thus, we can understand the disparagement in the following description :

"Faculty meetings never evoke stimulating discussions. Even routine matters are fumbled and puttered over in an amazingly incompetent way. By all who possess any first-hand knowledge of faculty meetings it is freely admitted that they are both discouragingly ineffective and intolerably dull." [40]

This same man goes on to add that one of the important reasons for this ineffectiveness is that faculties in America have no real authority. The professors realize that theirs is not really the responsibility for decisions of the first magnitude. "Their talks are not instruments leading to action but ends in themselves, with the natural result that they become showy, exaggerated, and sophistical."*

---

* Dr. C. C. Little has very definite views concerning the effectiveness of ordinary faculty meetings. He would do away with them! "Judging by past records, the faculty as an organized unit is not a safe or wise body to initiate academic policies or to decide upon their value en masse. Therefore, faculty meetings to discuss matters of policy should not be held." In its place he would inaugurate a small executive committee, representing all ranks. "There would probably be among the members of any large faculty, eight or ten emotionally balanced normal executives available to serve creditably on such a committee."

The Awakening College, Norton, 1930, p. 144.

Cf. "The Faculty Meeting and Democracy," J. P. Williams. Bull. of the American Association of University Professors, XXIV, 418, 1938.

The foregoing variations in attitude toward the academic life are based upon both objective and subjective factors. Objectively, it is obvious that the circumstances under which various professors function are not identical. Some, for example, may teach fifteen hours a week, others only half as much; some may serve on many committees, others on none. However, the subjective factor immediately intrudes itself into the analysis, for personality is a factor of selection in the constitution of one's environment. Even in the same college the environmental circumstances of different members of the faculty are likely to vary somewhat with regard to hours of preparation, committee work, departmental relations, and many other matters. The personality of the professor is definitely related to such variables. In addition, some academicians are better adjusted to the academic environment than others and this factor is very important in explaining differences in the foregoing interpretations. The well-adjusted professor is likely to grow expansive and optimistic whenever he contemplates his profession. The maladjusted one, on the other hand, grows querulous and lives in a disgruntled state. It is a truism of social psychology that the attitudes of the individual define his life-situation.

REFERENCES

SALARY

[1] Excerpt from *College Humor.*
[2] *Forum,* XVI, 98, 1983.
"The Pay of American College Professors," W. R. Harper.
[3] *Scribner's,* XXII, p. 629, 1897.
"Confessions of a College Professor."
[4] *Scribner's,* XXII, 512, 1897.
"Life of a College Professor," Bliss Perry.
[5] *World's Work,* VII, 4390, 1903.
"Pay of Teachers."
[6] *World's Work,* IX, 5455, 1904
"The College Year."
[7] *Atlantic Monthly,* XCV, 647, 1905.
"What Should College Professors be Paid?"
[8] *Nation,* LXXXIV, 212, 1907.
Editorial.
[9] *Literary Digest,* XXXVII, 119, 1908.
"Pay of College Professors."
[10] *American Magazine,* LXXXVIII, 15, 1919.
"Are Cheap Teachers going to be Good for your Children."
[11] *Century,* XCIX, 404, 1920.
"The Perplexities of a Professor."
[12] *Literary Digest,* LXIX, 27, 1921.
"Impoverished College Teaching."
[13] *Literary Digest,* XCIII, 30, 1927.
"Underpaid Teachers and Under-paying Students."
[14] *Literary Digest,* XCII, 29, 1927.
"Minimum Wages for Professors."
[15] *New Outlook,* CLXI, 39, 1932.
"The Crisis in the Ph. D.", Cedric Fowler.
[16] *Nation,* CXXXVIII, 349, 1934.
"The Plight of Higher Education," O. G. Villard.
[17] *Nation,* LXXXVIII, 524, 1909.
"Instructors' Wages."
[18] *Nation,* LXXXIX, 204, 1909.
"The Instructor."
[19] *Atlantic Monthly,* CXXIV, 232, 1919.
"Family Finances of a Young Professor."
[20] *Nation,* CXIII, 3, 1921.
"College Professors' and Instructors' Salaries."
[21] *Nation,* CXXXVII, 1933.
"The College Instructor," W. B. Thomas.

[22] *Forum,* XCIII, 88, 1935.
"Poor Professors," Ann Carter.
[23] See No. 2.
[24] *Nation,* LXXX, 129, 1905.
"College Tuition Fees."
[25] *Forum,* XCIX, 305, 1938.
"The Plight of the Professor's Wife," Norah Clancy.
[26] *Nation.* CXV, 597, 1922.
"The Professor's Wife."
[27] *Harper's.* CXXVI, 782, 1912.
"The Professor," Henry Canby.
[28] *Nation,* LXXX, 129, 1905.
"College Tuition Fees."
[29] *Popular Science,* LXXXII, 556, 1913.
"The American College as it Looks from the Inside," C. H. Handschin
[30] *World's Work,* III, 1737, 1901.
"Plain Words on Teachers' Wages."
[31] See No. 5.
[32] See No. 9.
[33] *Harper's.* CXXXIX, 106, 1919.
"The Colleges and the Nation," A. T. Hadley.
[34] *World's Work.* XXXVIII, 624, 1919.
"Universities from Within," A. L. Lowell.
[35] *American Magazine,* LXXXVIII, 15, 1919.
"Are Cheap Teachers Good for your Children?"
[36] See No. 12.
[37] See No. 22.
[38] *Forum,* LXXIV, 491, 1925.
"Fifty Thousand Dollars for Professors," Frank Bohn.
[39] See No. 7.
[40] *Nation,* CXXX, 130, 1930.
"Rats and Professors."
[41] *World's Work,* XIII, 8776, 1907.
"Autobiography of a College Professor," H. W. Rolfe.
[42] *New Republic,* LX, 286, 1929.
"A Wooden Horse for the Professors."
[43] *Saturday Evening Post,* CC, 26, 1927.
"The Professor Lot."
[44] *Nation,* CIV, 537, 1917.
"The Well-paid College Professor."
[45] *American Magazine,* LXXXIX, 54, 1920.
"Snickers at my Second-hand Clothes."
[46] *Scribner's,* LXXXVI, 1929.
"Foraging on Parnassus."

[47] *Scribner's,* LXXXV, 217, 1929.
"The Spirit of the Game," H. W. Whicker.
[48] *Harper's,* CLXVIII, 458, 1934.
"Faculty Wives," George Belane.
[49] *Collier's,* XXXV, 1905.
"Pensions for Professors."
[50] *Outlook,* LXXXIII, 120, 1906.
"Mr. Carnegie's Gift to the Teachers," H. S. Pritchett.
[51] *Nation,* LXXX, 394, 1905.
"Living Wages for Professors."
[52] *Saturday Evening Post,* CLXXIX, 20, 1906.
"Pensions for Professors."
[53] *North American Review,* CLXXXVI, 213, 1907.
"Advancement of Teaching," J. Jastrow.
[54] *North American Review,* CLXXXI, 1905.
"A Pension Fund for College Professors," C. F. Thwing.
[55] *Nation,* XCIX, 1914.
"The Professor's Compensation," H. S. Koopman.
[56] *Nation,* XC, 205, 1910.
"Carnegie Foundation and its Pension System."
[57] *Independent,* LXXIX, 7, 1914.
"Carnegie Foundation."
[58] *Literary Digest,* XLIX, 23, 1914.
"Carnegie's Attitude toward the Religious College."
[59] *Independent,* LXXXIII, 361, 1915.
"Ten Years of the Carnegie Pensions," H. S. Pritchett.
[60] See No. 53.
[61] *Independent,* LXIII, 1056, 1907.
"Carnegie Foundation for the Advancement of Teaching," C. F. **Thwing.**
[62] *New Republic,* XX, 383, 1919.
[63] *Atlantic Monthly,* CXXII, 737, 1918.
"Pension Problem and its Solution," H. S. Pritchett.
[64] *Atlantic Monthly,* CXXIV, 819, 1919.
"Mr. Carnegie's Service to the Teacher," H. S. Pritchett.
[65] *Nation,* CVIII, 158, 1919.
"The Academic Unrest," J. Jastrow.
[66] *Nation,* CVIII, 862, 1919.
"A Complacent Foundation," J. Jastrow.
[67] *Nation,* LXXXIII, 406, 1906.
Editorial.
[68] *Collier's,* LXV, 7, 1920.
[69] *Nation,* LXXXIV, 212, 1907.
Editorial.
[70] *Ladies Home Journal,* XXXVII, 24, 1920.

"Lo, the Poor School-teacher."
[71] See No. 22.
[72] *Nation*, CII, 41, 1916.
  "Pay of Professors."

REFERENCES

Academic Life

[1] *Saturday Evening Post*, CC, p. 26, 1927.
  "The Professor's Lot."
[2] *Harper's*, CXLI, p. 102, 1920.
  "On the Luxury of Being a Professor."
[3] *Atlantic Monthly*, CXXI, p. 218, 1918.
  "Why Teach?", Robert M. Gay.
[4] *Nation*, CIV, p. 537, 1917.
  "The Well-paid Professor."
[5] *American Mercury*, XLIV, 276, 1938.
  "Professors have Soft Jobs," Anonymous.
[6] *Nation*, LXXXVI, 1908.
  "College Grindstone."
[7] *New Republic*, XXII, p. 352, 1920.
  "Professors' Wives," Karen Jones.
[8] See No. 1 above.
[9] *Nation*, CXIII, p. 537, 1921.
  "The Genus Professor," Max McConn.
[10] *Scribner's*, XXII, p. 512, 1897.
  "The Life of a College Professor," Bliss Perry.
[11] *North American Review*, CCXIV, p. 21, 1921.
  "Teaching versus Business."
[12] *Scribner's*, LXXXVII, p. 90, 1930.
  "The Professor and his Wife," Ruth Brooks.
[13] *Atlantic Monthly*, XCVIII, p. 368, 1906.
  "Confessions of an Obscure Teacher."
[14] *Scribner's*, LX, p. 639, 1916.
  "Lo, the Poor Professor."
[15] See No. 12 above.
[16] See No. 7 above.
[17] See No. 12 above.
[18] See No. 1 above.
[19] See No. 1 above.
[20] See No. 5 above.
[21] *Atlantic Monthly*, LXXXIX, 1902.
  "College Professor and the Public," Bliss Perry.

[22] *Harper's,* CXXVI, p. 782, 1912.
"The Professor," Henry S. Canby.
[23] *Century,* XCIX, p. 404, 1920.
"The Perplexities of a Professor."
[24] *Leslie's Monthly,* XLIII, p. 141, 1897.
[25] *Harper's,* CXL, p. 249, 1920.
"Why I Remain in Industry."
[26] See No. 10 above.
[27] See No. 5 above.
[28] *Atlantic Monthly,* CXXXVII, p. 320, 1926.
"To a Young Man Bent on Entering the Professoriat," George Boas.
[29] See No. 25 above.
[30] *Forum,* XVII, p. 148, 1894.
"American Universities and the Training of Teachers," G. S. Hall.
[31] See No. 25 above.
[32] *Harper's,* CLXVIII, p. 458, 1934.
"Faculty Wives," George Belane.
[33] *Liberty,* Sept. 16, 1933.
"What Price Education," John Erskine.
[34] *Atlantic Monthly,* CLVI, p. 210, 1935.
"Twilight of the Professors," E. J. Goodspeed.
[35] *Forum,* XXXIII, 1902.
"Degradation of the Professorial Office," G. T. Ladd.
[36] *Forum,* LI, p. 321, 1914.
"The Professorial Quintain," F. B. R. Hellems.
[37] See No. 5 above.
[38] See No. 33 above.
[39] *American Mercury,* II, 1924.
"Pedagogue: Old Style," J. M. Cain.
[40] *New Republic,* X, 69, 1917.
"Faculty Meetings."

He thought he saw the naked Truth
Come to him in a dream.
"It is suppressed desire," he cried,
And gave a startled scream.
"Swear you are not," he said entranced,
"As lovely as you seem."

—Marion Calkins in the
New Republic.

CHAPTER III

Academic Freedom

It should be stated at once that the data falling under this heading are, with few exceptions, written from one point of view. Attempts to clarify the meaning of the concept, academic freedom, protests against dismissals, criticisms of administrative high-handedness and oath laws—in the discussion of all of these subjects the magazines, for the most part, are non-conservative.* It is not the author's purpose to take sides on this issue, however. His is the task of analyzing the data, developing their implications, and interpreting the whole problem sociologically.

DEFINITIONS

Let us begin with definitions. In the first place, the concept includes more than the faculty. "Academic freedom" encompasses the students as well. Yet in the pages which follow attention is focused upon the problem only as it relates to the professor. How can we define "academic freedom" as it affects him? Does it imply that the professor has, or should have, unlimited scope in his work? Are there to be no restricting influences? If complete and absolute freedom is not involved in the definition, who shall exercise a controlling influence and within what limits? These are comprehensive and significant issues. Let us see what light the periodical writers can throw upon the matter of definition.

A recent writer defines academic freedom as "the right of the teacher to say what he thinks."[1] This grants unlimited freedom to the professor. There are no restrictions contemplated apparently. No matter how biased by emotional factors the teacher

---

* "Non-conservative" is used in preference to "liberal," "progressive," or "radical," all three of which are likely to carry various emotional connotations. Our term, of course, is broad and inevitably vague.

may become in the course of his life-experience, his right to full and free expression shall be inviolate. Yet such is not the intent of this definition. Far from anarchistic, he hastens to add that,

"All freedom, academic or otherwise, is limited; no right can exist unless it is balanced by a duty. . . . For liberty, especially intellectual liberty, without responsibility is anarchy."

Thus, academic freedom is, according to this statement, limited by the teacher's sense of responsibility. But what is this? He asserts that criticism is the "essence of the teacher's responsibility" and by criticism he means the judicial variety. Judicial criticism, as opposed to destructive or constructive criticism, is a "search for truth without prejudice toward either side of a controversy." The teacher, that is to say, should not become an advocate. His task is not to find the answers to the problems discussed so much as "to sharpen the minds of the students so that they . . . will attack them with intelligence and with open minds."

"Responsibilities", and "rights" are complementary ethical concepts: my responsibility toward you indicates your right with regard to me. Thus, a social scientist feels that the teacher should take upon himself the responsibility to be judicial and that the trustees have a right to expect this of him.

"The trustees have a right . . . to require the professor to give both sides of social questions. . . . Again the trustees have a right to require the professor to devote most of his time in the classroom to the generally accepted facts and principles of his specialty." [2]

This is not the place to take up the whole issue of indoctrination, which has occupied the attention of educational theorists in recent years, but it may be said summarily that the judicial attitude definitely precludes indoctrination. Furthermore, the school as an integral part of the cultural pattern always tends to indoctrinate the young with currently accepted values. The *Nation* eschews the theory of indoctrination, pointing to the regimentation of thought in European dictatorships. The editor adds quite correctly that there is always more interference with academic freedom from the right than from the left and that "for the present the fight for academic freedom means primarily the fight for adequate recognition of the radical position."[3]

The college may avoid partisanship in other ways. Dr. Meiklejohn, after paying his respects to the judicial attitude, suggests another means of attaining the same end.

"A college faculty might be made up of many advocates, at least one advocate for every important line of popular thought and impulse, trusting to each to push his cause as strongly as he can."[4]

Thus, the college as a whole may be unprejudiced although no single professor may be. The assumption is that biases will cancel out in the interactional process. Apropos of this proposal Joseph Krutch has said:

"The defenders of free speech never professed to guarantee the sincerity of every speaker or to see to it that his position was genuinely disinterested. All they ever promised was to protect the right of opposing interests to answer . . ."[5]

"Freedom" is an elusive concept and already we may perceive diversities of definition. One view has it that academic freedom implies the judicial attitude while another seeks intellectual freedom through diversity of faculty opinion. A psychologist, H. C. Warren, adds another definition which, though not necessarily in conflict with the others, at least supplements them. He finds professorial autonomy to be the essence of academic freedom.

"Freedom of teaching, as scholars understand the term, means control of university instruction by the teaching profession itself, untrammeled by outside interference."[6]

The issue here is not the factor of control but the interference of those who are not professors. He implies that college professors should set up their own group control. The fact of social control is fundamental to group life everywhere. Even though professors were completely free from administrative control, the members of the faculty would exercise control in terms of the standards and ideals of scholarship and would very likely seek to remove those who deviated greatly from the academic *mores*. In this respect the academic group resembles all others, for all group life exists within the framework of social control whereby an effort is made to secure and maintain conformity of behavior and thought. The ideal of academic freedom, then, is a specific type of freedom and is limited by the ideals and purposes of the academic group. This is equally true of other kinds of freedom. Freedom of speech is not synonymous with freedom of action; political freedom is not economic freedom.

One important implication of this definition of academic freedom, involving the absence of constraint by non-academic forces, is that those who buy the service of college professors cannot prescribe its nature. This principle is frankly recognized by Professor Warren who warns that anything else encourages a hired-workman attitude toward the professor. On the contrary, he believes that the board of trustees should regard him as a trained expert responsible only to those in his field of endeavor.* This same attitude is voiced in the *Nation* in 1916 in a report of a special committee of the American Association of University Professors.

"University teachers should be understood to be, with respect to the decisions made and expressed by them, no more subject to the control of trustees, than are judges subject to the control of the President, with respect to the conclusions drawn." [7]

Several of the periodicals admit that full freedom gives those inclined to sensationalism a chance to function unfettered. Even the *Nation* asserts that "no doubt there are among the professorial body a certain number of foolish extremists, a certain number of shallow and sensational ranters."[8] In 1902 the *Literary Digest* reported an address by President Harper of the University of Chicago in which he criticized vigorously the sensational methods and undue loquacity of those professors who take advantage of their positions to propagate partisan views.[9] An editorial in the *Saturday Evening Post* in 1929 referred to professors who show a

---

* A valuable document for the student of this whole issue of academic freedom is the *Report of the Committee on Academic Freedom and Academic Tenure.* A.A.U.P. Bulletin, Vol. 1, Dec., 1915 (Reprinted in same bulletin, October, 1937). See also the article on "Academic Freedom" in the *Encyclopedia of the Social Sciences.* A. O. Lovejoy, the author, was the first secretary of the A.A.U.P.

contempt for the problems of college administration and even in a few instances seek to embarrass the administrative officers.

"There is a type of professor who attempts to be as silly, sensational, and shocking as possible. It is no wonder that presidents and trustees lose their patience now and then. In those rare instances when this patience does end, the public must not conclude rashly that the professor is a victim of narrow persecution or bigotry." [10]

While it is possible for non-conservatives to speak of the abuses of freedom, this point of view may easily be extended into a conservative theory of freedom which differentiates freedom and license. Apropos of this distinction, Howard Beale speaks of "fair-weather friends of freedom." These are the persons who talk of freedom within limits which means "freedom of another to hold his own views only so long as they are views which you regard as correct or unimportant." [12] *

Yet, is a professor free when he is under compulsion to say only the "right" things, that is, those which conform to the *mores?* It is true that individuals may experience no sense of restriction when their own attitudes happen to coincide with those dominant in the college and community. Psychologically, such individuals may have a sense of freedom. However, Randolph Bourne has said that it is the non-conformist who really tests the existence of freedom.

"Unless a university professor may hold opinions different from what the university as an institution holds, he is not intellectually free." [13]

Lest it be assumed that the non-conservative interpretation of academic freedom is held only by certain professors and magazine editors, a recent pronouncement by the Governor of Pennsylvania is given. As reported in the *New Republic,* Governor Earle stated in connection with the dismissal of Professor Turner from the University of Pittsburgh (1935):

---

* For a thorough examination of the issue of academic freedom with reference to the public schools, see H. K. Beale, *Are American Teachers Free?* Scribner's, 1936. This excellent volume is Part XII of the Report of the Commission on the Social Studies of the American Historical Association.

"Suppression of discussion is a violation of constitutional liberty, and will not be permitted in any institution which receives state aid and the support of the taxpayers of the state. . . . If the warning is not respected, I shall be forced to consider the University of Pittsburgh a private institution for the promotion of private interests entitled to no support from the Commonwealth . . ." [15]

A more conservative attitude toward freedom of teaching is expressed several times in the periodicals, though it is not common. During the investigation of a sociologist at the University of Missouri in 1930, a newspaper quoted in the *Literary Digest* stated:

"The public which puts up the money to support a school certainly has the right to supervision of what is done with the money." [14]

This attitude is directly opposed to that cited above which held that academic services should not be prescribed by those paying for them. This latter principle is commonly accepted with regard to the legal and medical professions but not with regard to education.

Academic freedom, however, does not apply only to the process of classroom instruction. Freedom in investigation is desired also. This is well brought out in the statement of principles passed by a conference of representatives of the following organizations in 1925 and reported upon by the *New Republic:* American Association of University Women, American Association of University Professors, the Association of American Colleges, the Association of American Universities, the Association of Governing Boards, the Association of Land Grant Colleges, the Association of Urban Universities, the National Association of State Universities, and the American Council on Education. The first point read as follows:

"A university or college may not place any restraint upon a teacher's freedom in investigation, unless restriction upon the amount of time devoted to it becomes necessary in order to prevent undue interference with teaching duties." [16]

Productive scholarship and research cannot flourish under any other conditions. This principle was expressed over forty years ago in the *Forum* by no less a research student than G. Stanley Hall, the President of Clark University. The real university professor, said he, working at remote outposts in the field of knowledge, must have the utmost freedom and "his individuality must be given the widest scope compatible with organization and harmony."[17] A recent writer, comparing the intellectual atmosphere in American universities and those of Europe, finds the former inferior.

"It is the task of thoughtful men to examine anew ideas on these topics (education, sex, religion, government, etc.) which tradition has handed down to us, to test them in the light of new experiences and of hitherto unknown facts which the changing social life presents. It is at this point that American universities seem to fail. . . . It is curious how little attention has been given to the smothering effect of such administrative control in American institutions of higher learning." [18] *

The aforementioned conference also stressed the principle that freedom in the exposition of one's subject extended not only to the classroom but to addresses and publications outside the college. In his role as trained expert the professor may be drafted for various kinds of public service beyond the confines of the college or university and here again he should be free from arbitrary external interference. On the other hand, there are several writers who do not feel that the professor can expect such a measure of freedom outside the classroom, even within his specialty. It is said that he should never forget in public utterances that he is part of an institution whose "good name" he can injure by "careless" and "reckless" statements.[19]

The conference further stated that no teacher may claim as his right the privilege of discussing in his classroom controversial topics outside of his own field of study. On this point, President Harper is in hearty agreement.

"A professor abuses his privilege of expression of opinion who, although a student, and perhaps an authority in one department or group of departments, undertakes to speak authoritatively on subjects which have no relation to the department in which he was appointed to give instruction." [20]

---

* "In all these domains of knowledge, the first condition of progress is complete and unlimited freedom to pursue inquiry and publish its results. Such freedom is the breath in the nostrils of all scientific activity." *Report of the Committee on Academic Freedom and Academic Tenure*, A.A.U.P. Dec. 1915, p. 14.

Similarly, outside the university, the conference decided the teacher need not be given unlimited fredom when speaking or writing beyond the scope of his own field.

"The teacher, in speaking or writing outside the institution upon subjects beyond the scope of his own field is entitled to precisely the same freedom and is subject to the same responsibility as attaches to all other citizens."

The limits of this freedom are patently vague, for the freedom of other citizens in this regard is ill-defined.

The Relation of Tenure to Freedom

Tenure guarantees freedom. The two problems are usually considered together. (Committee A of the A.A.U.P. is the committee on academic freedom and tenure.) The reason is that the professor really does not possess freedom unless he is assured of his position. That freedom is a mockery which cannot guarantee its possessor continuance in office. The professor seeks security of tenure along with freedom so that no board of trustees, legislature, nor president can justify dismissal with the sophistry that anyone may say what he pleases so long as he is willing to take the consequences.

Several years ago the *New Republic* referred to the "outrageous system of re-engaging the entire faculty each year."

"This means that in order to get rid of a teacher, it is only necessary not to reappoint him. Under these circumstances no one has any security of tenure." [21]

Under these circumstances, it may be added, no one has genuine academic freedom. Similarly, at the conference already mentioned several times, a recommendation was passed which implies that there is a close relationship between tenure and freedom.

"It is desirable that termination of a permanent or long-term appointment for cause should regularly require action by both a faculty committee and the governing board of the college. . . . In the trial of charges of professional incompetence the testimony of scholars in the same field, either from his own or from other institutions, should always be taken . . ."

The insistence upon trial before one's professional peers in the case of alleged incompetence indicates a suspicion that such charges, in reality, may conceal a question of academic freedom.

On the other hand, tenure protects the incompetent. President Conant of Harvard has said:

"We all know too many cases where a man once appointed for life to a professorship proceeds by slow degrees to betray his trust . . . he enjoys the security of his office and neglects all but the most formal duties." [22]

Another writer agrees that once a man receives a permanent appointment there is no way of displacing him, unless his inefficiency becomes scandalous. "It is the *reductio ad absurdum* of civil-service principles."[23] *

The Faculty and the Administration

It is not uncommon for the college and university to be likened to the business corporation. For instance, in connection with the dismissal of Professor Scott Nearing from the University of Pennsylvania, the chancellor of Syracuse University made the following comparison:

"That is what would happen to an editorial writer of the Tribune if he were to disregard the things for which the paper stands and write Bull Moose or Democratic politics into the Tribune because such was his conscience or conviction. Conscience is not an infallible guide . . . and convictions must be more than honest; they must be correct." [24]

He goes on to say that the board of trustees is the supreme authority and that, if it decides that the best interests of the university demand the professor's removal, he should go quietly. About the same time, the *Forum* carried a statement by a trustee of Northwestern University.

"In all things they (professors) should promptly and gracefully submit to the final determination of the trustees. A professor may be an advocate but his advocacy must be in harmony with the conclusions of the powers that be." [25]

Here is an issue of no mean importance. Could the American college and university be better administered by the faculty than by boards of trustees who do not pretend, as a rule, to be experts in educational philosophy? Should the faculty have a larger hand

---

* Cf. H. K. Beale, op. cit., p. 748.

in settling questions of expenditure as well as those of educational policy? Are we educating our college youth away from democratic ideals by the form of organization prevalent in our schools? These are matters of great moment to higher education.

"Shall the University become a Business Corporation?" is the title of an article written by the President of Massachusetts Institute of Technology in 1905 for the *Atlantic Monthly*.* Dr. Pritchett draws a contrast between European universities and those in America. In the former the watchword is freedom while the American university "has tended more and more to conform in its administration to the methods of the business corporation."[26] Recently Professor Laski has commented on the fact that most of the Harvard professors were not consulted about a successor to President Lowell. This is in striking contrast to the self-government at Oxford, Cambridge, and London.

"In England, Oxford and Cambridge are self-governing institutions; and both the Vice Chancellor and the heads of Houses are chosen by the teachers themselves. In London, the Vice Chancellor is elected by a Senate which is mainly a teaching body; and the heads of colleges are invariably chosen by committees in which representatives of the teachers sit. The general process of university government, moreover, is carried on by committees in which the professoriate invariably, and the younger teachers generally, have a share."[27]

In this connection we quote the remark of a German professor made in the course of introducing an American colleague to the German Emperor.

"Will your Majesty graciously receive our distinguished guest from the United States. He fitly bears the title of 'Exchange Professor,' since he comes from a monarchy within a republic to a republic within a monarchy."[28]

How may we account for this difference? Professor Dewey finds one reason in the remoteness of European universities from common affairs. While his own faith in the ultimate superiority of a system based upon an intimate connection of education and

---

* This whole subject is treated exhaustively by Thorstein Veblen in *The Higher Learning in America* (op. cit.), the subtitle to which reads, "A Memorandum on the Conduct of Universities by Business Men."

the common life is unmitigated, he is compelled to note that such remoteness "has a protective value for a certain kind of free intellectual life and has rendered possible the growth of independent standards of intellectual excellence."[29] Two writers refer to the legal factor. Arthur Livingston informs us that European law possesses the concept of property existing by itself without an owner; whereas in our legal tradition all property must have an owner.

"The donations left by our philanthropists are vested as property rights in trustees, recognized in law as virtual owners, and possessing, within testamentary restrictions, all the rights of owners." [30]

A second writer, who conceals his identity, points out that the civil law affirms that the corporation is the college and the professors mere employees.

"Any unbending attitude towards the faculty is understood on both sides to be that of the genial and kind-hearted master towards his servant. A matter of condescension, of courtesy, of free grace, and not at all moral right or necessity." [31]

There is the historical factor, also. The anonymous writer referred to in the preceding paragraph traces the history of our colleges and universities. These were established by ministers and for ministers. But the New England pastors were busy caring for their respective flocks, so they were forced to hire instructors to carry on their projected work of instruction. Another, writing five years before Veblen published his study of higher education, says that the origin of the governing board lies not in democracy but in theocracy. "Founded to educate ministers, our colleges had to be organized to guard against the creeping in of heresy."[32] Later on, control was shifted to the business man under the impact of our secularization and commercialism.*

Enough has been said to indicate that the view which regards the college or university as a business corporation has implications for academic freedom. Sumner refers to the strain toward consistency in the *mores*. At this point we may observe the intrusion

---

* Veblen, op. cit., Chapter 2.

of the economic *mores* upon education: the college is a corporation and its management is likely to be along those lines found to be most effective in the accumulation of profits, namely, strong leadership and a conception of the faculty as hired men. Certainly there is expressed in the foregoing analysis, directly and by implication, the attitude that the control of our institutions of higher learning is undemocratic. In the periodical literature one finds boards of trustees and presidents often called "rulers" and "absentee owners."* Dewey finds the corporate form of organization to be an obstacle to academic freedom but explains the presence of men of wealth on the boards as follows:

"It would be a matter of surprise were it otherwise, where education is in process of constant expansion which requires constant increase and profitable investment of funds." [33]

The fact of administrative control is not evaded by the administrators themselves. In 1917, for instance, a committee on academic freedom of the Association of American Colleges, consisting of four college presidents, presented a report that differed markedly from that of a similar committee of the American Association of University Professors. It declared that "the final authority with regard to the engaging or retention of teachers should be, not the students, or alumni, or even the faculty, but the trustees acting in conjunction with the president." The committee would willingly see an organization of professors determine the professional standing of colleagues under fire, but it would not allow such a decision of professional standing to determine executive action in all cases.[34]

It is frequently said of democracy that the people get as good a government as they deserve. Perhaps the same generalization applies to professors. In addition to the religious and commercial influences, there appear to be others tending in the direction of faculty subordination. Academic specialization is said to preclude greater faculty participation in administration. In 1900 a college

---

* On the other hand, the board of trustees at the University of Minnesota recently put itself on record as being very definitely in favor of academic freedom. *Cf. New Republic*, XCIV, 59, 1938.

president wrote of the perplexities of his office. On this point he gave the following opinion:

"A successful administrator will counsel with individual members of his faculty in all such matters, and may even call occasional meetings of the entire faculty in order that he may secure the advantage of general discussion and general expression; but the initiative and the final responsibility ought to lie with the executive. It is an absolute impossibility for a man to keep himself in the temper and enthusiasm of an investigator and instructor in one given line or subject and at the same time keep such full and complete touch with the outside world as to know exactly what administrative course is the wisest and safest to be pursued." [35]

If we accept, in some measure, the characterizations of the professor presented in Chapter 1, we have some further basis for an explanation of his institutionalized subordination. The habits of thought and action engendered by scholarly and pedagogical endeavors are hardly of a sort designed to win the confidence of administrators. If college teachers are addicted to pedantic details, it is not surprising that their administrative tasks are trivial. If they are impractical, those working out policies will not seek their counsel. Timid men will not excite the admiration of business men serving on governing boards. Academic writers admit these facts. Professor J. E. Kirkpatrick, writing in the *New Republic,* admits that professors are somewhat lacking in administrative experience and practical ability, that they have given themselves too exclusively to the study, the laboratory, and the lecture room. He believes, however, that the professor is capable of learning how to conduct the business of his institution.[36]

Yet do not the faculty members of every institution spend many hours in committee work? One professor, for example, when asked how he felt about academic freedom said that "all the academic freedom he wanted was freedom from committee meetings and a chance to go on with his work." Such committee tasks may account in part for the failure of American scholars to be more productive, suggested H. S. Pritchett in 1905. John Dewey looks for a deeper reason and finds it in the American culture.

"As long as chief prestige attaches in the American mind to outward signs of conspicuous activity rather than to scientific and artistic achievement, intellectual life will pay the price." [38]

Similarly, Laski writes of those academicians who love card-indexes, "soul-destroying committees, and the complicated intrigues for promotion or an increase in the departmental budget."[39]

In the face of such duties do professors desire greater participation in university government? The point is that these writers want the professor to have a real voice in the formulation of policies and not merely a greater burden of routine tasks carried out in a clerical manner. They seem to feel that there is a difference between committee work of a technical nature that never involves more than a few minor changes in the institution and a thorough consideration of matters of institutional policy. Here we may recall what was said about faculty meetings in the previous chapter. The triviality of these meetings signifies that important decisions are not made there. In many institutions such meetings are largely a gesture to democratic *mores* and, for some of the faculty, provide an opportunity for harmless amusement.*

As a matter of fact, the burden of administrative tasks is used by one writer as an argument for the separation of the faculty from the problems of administration:

"The business of university faculties is teaching. It is not legislation and it is not administration—certainly not beyond the absolute necessities. There is just complaint because the necessities of administration take much time from teaching." [40]

On the other hand, a larger group favors the extension of faculty participation. An anonymous academic writer proposed the following reform in 1918:

"What we need is a reconstitution of trustees and faculty as a single board, with such division of labor among them as is now managed by means of committees. In the reformed corporation, matters of finance would naturally be under the administration of the legal and business experts, scholastic matters under the care of those who now compose the faculty." [41]

It is not suggested by him that all professors should take an active part in administration but only those who show some ability along

---

* Too long for reproduction here is a satirical sketch by George Boas entitled, "Committee Report," *Harper's,* CLXII, 504, 1930.

this line. These, no doubt, would have to be relieved of at least a portion of their normal teaching duties. The author would like to make one comment on this proposal. It may sound equitable to allow scholastic matters to be handled by faculty representatives and financial matters by business men but the two will not separate so readily. If handling the finances means control over the distribution of funds among the various enterprises connected with the institution, then the business men possess an effective veto over the policies of any academic body. Those who control the budget are likely to be the real policymakers.

A second proposal is similar to the first. Professor Laski would like to see policies shaped by a committee upon which teachers had at least one-third of the representation. University appointments and promotions should be made by an academic body subject only to the approval of the governing body. "The tremendous hierarchy of the present academic structure should be abolished."[42] He further believes in permanence of tenure after a period of probation. If the academic group had charge of promotions, there would be a far larger number of critical treatises from the younger men. He asserts: "I believe that there is a basic incompatibility between academic freedom and the presidential system." A year later, in another magazine, Laski writes of "Self-determination for Faculties."

"A body of men like the teachers of Harvard, or Princeton, or Illinois ought not to have decisions made for them without an adequate part in their making. The present method is an external despotism which, even if it is on occasion benevolent, neglects essential sources of knowledge and opinion and ideas."[43]

Rather ironically, he suggests that it is at least possible that the faculty could have ideas of value to contribute. The inference is that, since the educational work of the institution is carried on by the teachers, they may have fruitful ideas on matters of policy.*

---

* "Administrators are comparatively out of contact with the actual work of the institution and hence are not in a position to see many of the serious problems and possibilities which arise in connection with instruction." Bull. of the A.A.U.P., XXII, 512, 1936.

Both of these writers base their proposals on a faith in democratic organization as the form best designed to promote the general welfare. They believe that the extension of democracy on the campus would improve the work of higher education.*

In the discussions of faculty participation in university government have the writers forgotten that many of the deans and a number of college presidents were teachers at one time? In such instances have these administrators not had an opportunity to develop the insight into teacher problems requisite to the sympathetic handling of faculty affairs? Let us examine this matter. In the first place, there is at work in every college or university a continuous process of selection whereby certain individuals succeed in the struggle for administrative positions and others fail. Dean McConn describes one type likely to succeed, calling him "Professor Up-to-date-icus."

"He is unquestionably a mongrel formed by unnatural crossing of the Genus Professor with the entirely distinct genus of Business Man. . . . Open the university catalogue to the list of faculty committees and take off the names which occur three times or oftener. For the Professors Up-to-date-icus are the mainstays of the committees. . . . He runs a big department. . . . Through it all he remains a cheery optimist, hail-fellow-well-met, one hundred percent American. . . . Is it any wonder the honors of deanship and presidency seek him out?" [44]

Another goes farther in the way of evaluation and asserts that the universities have been molded, not by intellectual pioneers, but by "humdrum minds with so-called 'administrative' ability, men who conceived it as their highest ambition to become a dean or a president rather to excel in thought or writing."[45] In addition to selection there is the process of adjustment to be considered. We all tend to adjust ourselves to our environments. This process involves rationalization of attitude and the acquisition of new behavior patterns.

---

* We are concerned only with faculty problems. Yet there are other aspects to educational democracy such as student participation in the determination of educational policy. It is characteristic of groups and individuals to seek for themselves that which they deny to others. Thus, in the classroom there may be a little evidence of democracy, although the autocratic teacher becomes indignant over the autocracy of the president.

"Power corrodes the head and dulls imaginative insight. For power always searches for routine and when the academic politician becomes a university president, there is nothing he subconsciously fears as a genuinely inventive mind." [46]

Thus, even assuming that the dean or president who has come up from the teaching ranks once had an intimate contact with the professorial mind, it usually happens that the new role and status tend to develop blind spots. This process of adjustment to institutional requirements is not peculiar to the academic man become administrator and the author could, if it were relevant, analyze in the same terms the institutional blind spots of the professor in his relations to students.

As already mentioned, most of the articles urge some modifications in the existing organization of higher learning. We have had occasion, however, to present the administrator's point of view, especially the argument of the inabilities resultant from academic specialization. Several other articles express a sympathetic attitude toward the problems of the college president. One, written by a president's widow, emphasizes the lack of cooperation on the part of professors.

"A man may enter the presidency with the highest ideals of working with his faculty in the spirit of cooperation and harmony, but unless he is associated with a body of men, each one of whom is a gentleman of honor, as well as a scholar, having breadth and wisdom to see that his own interests cannot always be forwarded at the expense of some other department . . . a president cannot continue his work along his chosen lines. When a college faculty can be found that is imbued with such wisdom, we shall have the ideal institution needing no personal domination." [47]

Another article expresses a favorable attitude toward the appointment of professors by the president. The latter, he says, is not like the members of the faculty who fear competition. If professors have the task of recommending appointments, they will prefer docile mediocrity to men of ability sufficient to develop into rivals for the positions that they hold. [48]

METHODS AND AGENCIES OF CONTROL

Since it appears that the professor is in a position of subordination in the typical college or university, we may inquire concerning the means of control exercised by the powers that be. One of the least conspicuous methods is that of selecting "safe" men for faculty posts. Harvard has been accused of employing this method of faculty control.

"Mr. Lowell has boasted in public that Harvard had never dismissed an instructor for his views; he is understood to believe that if a university exercises proper care in selecting its professors, dismissals will never be necessary." [49] *

Dismissal is another method of control, exercised in comparatively few instances, but likely to be given a great deal of publicity. The *New Republic,* editorializing upon the University of Pittsburgh incident of 1935, stated that "Chancellor Bowman boasts that in his first year at the university, 1921, he dismissed fifty-three members of the faculty." [50] In criminology a distinction is made between specific and general deterrence. The former means deterrence of the offender, the latter refers to the general effect upon the group. Dismissals may be compared to capital punishment, so far as specific deterrence is concerned. The offending professor has his head chopped off, so to speak, and can do no further "harm", at least at the institution in question. General deterrence may occur, however. Twenty years ago a professor told of the effect of a dismissal on the faculty. All summer long most of the faculty felt depressed. Fear grew as did the belief that to get ahead one would have to truckle and pull wires. There was no enthusiasm for work in September and all reported a diminution in loyalty to the institution. [51]

Short of discharge, pressure of various kinds may be brought to bear upon the culprit. Too often it is assumed that, if the professor retains his job, he has won the battle with the authorities. Tenure means the hold which one has on one's job but there are other considerations. Promotions may be delayed or refused; in

---

* Cf. Norman Foerster, *The American State University,* Univ. of North Carolina Press, 1937, pp. 166-169.

fact, demotion may take place. Mr. Beale states that "dismissals are relatively unimportant anyway. The threat of dismissal is just as effective." In view of the timidity of teachers, he believes that threats are especially effective. Ostracism may be effected by techniques best known to those involved. Appropriations for assistance or equipment may be cut to the bone. Privileges may be withdrawn. Opprobrious labels may be attached to his name.

"Through many insidious channels the impression may be conveyed that they are 'unsafe', 'unsound', 'unscientific'. The great advantage of so stigmatizing a man is that it relieves one from the necessity of combatting with fact and argument his teachings—a task which might be considerably difficult." [52]

It is interesting to watch the career of the radical in the ordinary college or university. Before long he is flinging himself into the political or industrial struggle, publishes works that call into question traditional attitudes and practices, and teaches without reserve the faith that is in him.

"At first he is let alone; but as his tendencies become potent, pressure begins from within and without. It may come in delicate intimations, in remonstrances, or in reprimands; it can range from hint to dismissal." [53]

In accounting for the control exercised over the faculty, the administration cannot be held wholly responsible. Institutionalized leaders are subject to the influences of public opinion and pressure. Just as our judges and laws reflect public attitudes, so the attitude of the governing board toward academic freedom may be an integral part of the *mores* of the community. With sociological insight President Hadley of Yale wrote as follows:

"The fact seems to be that the form of corporate control chosen makes far less difference with the degree of freedom of the teacher than does the general habit or standard of the community concerning toleration." [54]

Yet, aside from the sanction given to the authority of the administrative officers, the community may take a more active part in stamping out heterodoxy. A pillar in a certain community told a professor that, so long as he remained a member of the faculty, he was not to consider himself a citizen and therefore he had no right to express an opinion that might be displeasing to *bona fide* citizens. This man was not connected with the university in any way but he reflected, according to the professor writing the article, the attitude of a large number of voters.[55] An editor tells of attending a dinner shortly after the World War at which occasion the operations of the local *vigilantes* were revealed. One lady remarked that she had attended a dinner to which a number of young instructors had been invited. "Do you know, they were all Bolsheviks?" she said. The silence was broken by a prosperous business man of the community who remarked,

"It is too bad that it is that way. But it is true and we are meeting the situation. We are keeping a watch on these people and are gradually having them dismissed from the university but not on that ground, of course." [56]

The editor was told that, at the same university, faculty men had been followed about town and stenographers sent by a business men's organization had taken down their speeches. These were the days of the "Big Red Scare" and the country was fearful of radicalism.

The alumni can and do bring pressure upon the administration. Percy Marks, writing in *Harper's* in 1926, labels them the "Pestiferous Alumni." The amount of alumni interference is enormous. Presidents and deans must exercise a lot of patience in listening to their complaints and suggestions for old Alma Mater.

"The alumni interfere about everything and their interference is not only a fiendishly irritating itch that cannot be scratched but a serious drawback to the college as well." [57]

Well-aroused over the intrusions of the alumni, he adds that the lack of academic freedom is due more to them than to the trustees. Another writer, calling himself Alumnus, exhorts his fellow-alumni to contribute money and come back to visit their alma maters but "let them be willing to have the men who taught them do the same for their sons without their interference."[58]

State legislatures have engaged in heresy-hunting from time to time. An academic writer claims that the state university held out some promise at one time of establishing democratic control in education.

"But unfortunately the state university has patterned itself on the only American model it had—the parental foundational type. In it the parent and the millionaire are replaced by the legislative majority." [59]
In 1925 Ohio provided for an investigation, the intent of which was to drive out of the state-supported institutions any teachers of radical proclivities. A resolution was passed which provided that:

"No part of the money appropriated for the support of state colleges or schools shall be paid to any teacher thereof who has been publicly active in any socialist, atheist, communist, or other organization of revolutionists or who is known to be a member of a body whose teachings have encouraged efforts to overthrow the government of the United States." [60]

In 1930 the *New Republic* carried an article on the spoils system in college, being an account of Governor Bilbo and higher education in Mississippi. The governor forced hosts of dismissals in the three major state educational institutions in order to punish his political enemies and reward his friends.

" 'Boys' said Theodore G. Bilbo, 'We've just hung up a new record. We've bounced three college presidents and made three new ones in the record time of two hours'. . . . It was a declaration of war upon the immunity of education from political influence and corruption, a war which has already cost 179 faculty members of the state university and colleges their positions." [61]

Academic freedom in Mississippi, the article concludes, has become a memory and a hope. In this connection we add the suggestion of another writer that the privately endowed college or university is in a position to enrich our intellectual life "by harboring men whose ideas are valuable but a little too hot for the publicity supported institution to handle safely and comfortably."[62] But while the private schools may avoid political control, are they immune from the influences of wealth and religious conviction?

All of us of voting age will recall the Scopes trial and anti-evolutionary legislation. In 1921 the *Nation* had written ironically of "teacher-baiting: the new sport" in connection with a loyalty oath law enacted in Oklahoma.[63] By the middle of the decade the new sport was enjoying popularity in a number of state legislatures where anti-evolutionary laws were introduced. *Forum* gave its readers the law enacted in Tennessee, the state that acquired world notoriety for its fight against Darwinism.

"An act prohibiting the teaching of the evolution theory in all universities, normal, and other public schools of Tennessee . . .

Section 1. Be it enacted by the general assembly of the State of Tennessee that it shall be unlawful for any teacher in any of the universities . . . and all other public schools which are supported in whole or in part by public funds . . . to teach any theory that denies the story of the Divine creation of man as taught in the Bible, and to teach instead that man has descended from a lower order of animals.

Section 2. Be it further enacted that any teacher found guilty of the violation of this act . . . shall be fined not less than $100 nor more than $500 for each offense." [64]

A bill to repeal this law was introduced six years later (1931) but failed of passage.[65] Mr. James I. Finney, editor of the Nashville Tennessean, predicted that in time the law would be repealed but added the following comment:

"The day will be delayed as long as the enemies of the statute base their hostility to it on their contempt for the religious faith of our people. The law will go only when its repeal will not be interpreted as a triumph for the skeptics, agnostics, and would-be defenders of our material civilization." [66]

Other states passed or tried to pass anti-evolutionary legislation, although the periodicals give no complete account.

The most recent attempt on the part of legislatures (which have been influenced in their action by various so-called patriotic types of pressure groups) to curb free expression of thought in the schools and colleges of the country is the oath law for teachers. The *Literary Digest* gives a sample of such an oath.

"I do solemnly swear, or affirm, that I will support the Constitution of the United States, the Constitution of the State of ——— and the laws enacted thereunder, and that I will teach, by precept and example, respect for the flag, reverence for law and order, and undivided allegiance to the Government of our country, the United States of America." [67]

Such an oath, it is said, must be taken by teachers and professors in twenty states, seven states having enacted oath laws in the legislative sessions of the year (1935) despite the opposition of non-conservative groups.

Such laws find very little support in the general magazines. Many criticize them vigorously and even periodicals of a conservative outlook express opposition. The editor of the *Saturday Evening Post* is in favor of weeding out those who lack the essentials of patriotism in view of the signs of radicalism among teachers. What grounds does the profession have for becoming disturbed over these laws, he asks. Legislators and judges have long been required to take such an oath. Yet he doubts if the remedy lies in the teacher's oath law.

"If a man or woman lacks the essentials of patriotism and of honor, he or she will take but will not keep an oath. . . . If the situation in any college or in any community is not sound, it is up to the constituents of the particular institution or school system to correct it." [68]

Professor Carl Becker, in citing his own experience, expresses doubts concerning the efficacy of oath-made patriotism. In accordance with the law in his state, he was requested to sign a statement affirming his support to federal and state constitutions.

"After reading this statement carefully, I signed it, willingly, and without resentment. I always wish to conform to the laws, and in this instance there was no difficulty in doing so, since this law, so far as I could see, neither deprived me of any rights that I formerly had nor imposed upon me any duties not already imposed. . . . What then does the Ives law mean? . . . So far as I can see, nothing except this: that teachers in New York State are obliged to acknowledge in writing that they are obligated by the obligations imposed upon them by the duties they have assumed, and by the obligations imposed upon all citizens by the Constitution of the United States and the Constitution of the State of New York." [69]

However, the well-known historian adds that he considers it part of the duty of his position to say frankly that the legislators of New York have made a mistake in passing such legislation.

Yet it is not the content of the oaths that constitutes the problem, according to Carl J. Friedrich, writing in *Harper's*. Many of them, he admits, are innocuous enough. "It is the principle implied in any such oath that teaching is a form of propaganda." [70] Evidently, he feels that the administration of such oaths will, in actual practice, strengthen the hand of the strongly conservative forces in the country who are likely to be encouraged in their vigilance over teachers by the passage of these laws. Thus, academic freedom will suffer. Mr. Friedrich suggests a further thought:

"It is depressing to realize that the oath has always cropped up as a political device when the political order was crumbling."

The upsurge of sentiment in favor of loyalty oath laws has been due in considerable measure to the recent depression. During periods of economic reverses radical sentiment is likely to increase. Even those of a customarily conservative viewpoint may begin to wonder about the validity of the economic *mores* and institutions, for crises induce thinking where formerly there had been unreflective adherence to the traditional ways. Such a development is likely to be opposed by those enthusiastic defenders of the *status quo* who mobilize their forces to combat the new "menace." It is not necessary to suggest that the political order is "crumbling." The recent oath laws seem to have resulted from the fears of conservatives that our constitutions of learning are being perverted, and our social order undermined, by the furtive activities of radicals. However, the *Nation* thinks that the cloud of loyalty laws may have a silver lining for American liberals, for such laws may awaken professors, who might otherwise be complacent, to the unpleasant realization that it can happen here. In an editorial headed "Bombing Out the Middle Class," this periodical endeavors to be optimistic:

"Viewed pragmatically, teachers' oaths may prove a most effective weapon in the current fight for human rights, bringing to the front several divisions which might have preferred to sit tight in academic dugouts in a hundred university towns. To many persons, especially students and teachers, the oaths have appeared as a startling symbol of repression . . ."[71]

Finally, paradoxical as it may seem, the professors themselves constitute a force pitted against academic freedom. In 1937 a professor writes that he has been driven to the conclusion that "with few exceptions the professors themselves were the greatest enemies of academic freedom." He states that one of the cherished illusions of college professors is their identification with the ruling classes and that most of them manifest intellectual standpatism.

"Nervous daughters of the American Revolution to the contrary notwith-standing, there are no more stodgy defenders of the status quo than our university faculties. . . . Most of the professors in America are engaged in a tiresome elaboration of the obvious and fiercely resent any innovation of method or content." [72]

He believes that the academic man needs complete freedom of thought if he is to fulfil his proper function and concludes significantly that "that freedom must be protected, even from the professor himself." In this connection the question naturally arises: how can the general public be expected to appreciate the ideal of academic freedom when the most educated elements, themselves in the academic profession, do not seem to grasp its meaning?

THE EFFECTS OF RESTRICTION

What effects do these restrictions have upon the teacher, the investigator, the students, and democratic society at large? Most of the magazines discussing this aspect of the question come to the conclusion expressed by a French sociologist in the *Literary Digest* at the beginning of the century.

"If a professor is to do the highest grade of work and accomplish a maximum amount of good, he must be at liberty to think and speak as he pleases, even though his thoughts and opinions may be contrary to those of trustees and founders. In America, unfortunately, this is not yet the case." [73]

Bitter and satirical are the remarks of a writer in the *Century*. He cites humorous examples of academic repression: three professors resigning under fire for insinuating to students that the stork theory was open to doubt, one professor dismissed for alleging the existence of sex in plant life.

"The situation at Mount Mump is considerably cleared by the dropping of professors Grind and Digger, the first for absent-mindedly appearing in class without his muzzle, and the second for permitting an undergraduate to think." [74]

Do we not look to the colleges and universities for the preservation of high intellectual ideals? Is not an institution practicing repression defeating itself by compromising the purposes that justify its existence? The periodicals give a mighty affirmation.

Teachers and scholars are looked upon as the custodians of the noble traditions of science and learning. The professor, it is further asserted, cannot remain a true scholar and do the work which society demands if he is relegated to the position of an hireling. As a matter of fact, no one can do the best grade of thinking who must keep one eye focussed upon the limits of his tether while the other observes the problem at hand. (This principle applies also to the classroom in the relations of the student to the dogmatic, authoritative teacher.) Single-mindedness is an essential condition for reflection of high calibre. It is refreshing to read the remarks of Dr. Meiklejohn on this point.

"Professors must be good men, must study well, and teach successfully. If these requirements are met, no question can be raised regarding their opinions." [75]

But the editor of the *Nation* sorrowfully reports that, in reality, we get only a "treadmill culture labelled preparation for life. The faculties have been so long in servitude that they hardly agree about what should be taught or how teaching should be done."[76]

What of the students? Does the principle of academic freedom rest on a larger foundation than the rights of professors?

"The question touches deeply the whole spirit of university life. Even more for the sake of the students than for that of the professors, the intellectual integrity and independence of the professoriate must be upheld." [77]

What confidence, asks another, can the students have in their instructors in social science if they know that those instructors are subject to the American Legion or other espionage and censorship? All honor and influence go from the vocation of teaching.

"All the students cease to learn, or to be lead, but only jest at the comic wobblings of the despicable hireling before them." [78]

An atmosphere of repression may become a criterion of selection. The courageous non-conformists, especially if they are persons of ability who can obtain positions elsewhere, beat a hasty exodus at the earliest opportunity, leaving the rest behind to endure the adverse situation. This selectivity has been observed many times.*

---

*Cf. E. Y. Hartshorne, *German Universities and National Socialism*, Harvard Univ. Press, 1937.

Of course, it must be remembered that there are many professors who, because of the nature of their fields, are not directly concerned with the problem of academic freedom. These may remain without incurring the charge of timidity or truckling. The selectivity goes on particularly in the fields dealing with issues of immediate social import. Moreover, the factor of repression may be selective in the profession in general, keeping out many young men and women of first-class potentiality.

"It seems fair to the professor, however, to suggest that his office will be much more attractive to the stronger and more able men if he is given more responsibility in the administration of the university. Men of this type needed as teachers are not attracted by the menial position now held by the professor. For, in spite of his brave talk in the classroom and his brilliant robes, flaunted on the campus occasionally, the professor is a servant in his own house." [79] *

PROFESSIONAL ORGANIZATION

During the second decade of the present century we find the first signs of agitation in the periodicals for organization. In 1911 the *Literary Digest* published excerpts from a study of academic ethics by John Chapman under the title of "Rabbit-like Professors."

"The average of this species will look on at an act of injustice done to a brother professor by their college president with the same unconcern as the rabbit who is not attacked watches the ferret pursue his brother up and down the warren to predestinate and horrible death." [80]

This writer thinks that the professor should make some effort to protect himself and his colleagues. Several years later the academic man is excoriated for his lack of spirit in the face of intimidation and repression. Writing under the title of "The Third American Sex" George Cook describes the American scholar as a pitiable figure who is not even mentioned in articles and books dealing with college life. The professor's instinct of self-preservation has triumphed over original and courageous thought and thus the students are indifferent to him, regarding his courses simply as credits. Of course, he states ironically, they are perfectly free to

* Cf. W. W. Waller, *The Sociology of Teaching*, Wiley, 1932, 453-55.

hold any opinions they please so long as they do not express them. No one knows how many fine minds have succumbed to the pressure from the governing boards. "The slow death in them of the higher life of the mind is the silent tragedy of our university life."

What does he propose? Unionization is the only line of action that can emancipate the professor.

"Shrinking instinctively from the application of the working class method to their profession, the academic workers have failed to consider seriously the only line of action likely to lead to their independence. . . . It is perhaps because we are not accustomed to look to them for anything requiring so much guts as the formation of a union that the two ideas 'professor' and 'union' clash. But 'union' is capable of taking 'professor' out of the category of the ridiculous." [81]

While timidity and academic snobbery may account in part for the reluctance of the profession to organize there seem to be other factors not included in this analysis. One of these is the presence of the monastic ideal which is opposed to emphasis upon materialistic considerations. Another element in the situation is probably the individualism of the professor. As a matter of fact, an academic writer essayed to answer Mr. Cook in which both of these factors were mentioned.[82]

In 1915 the American Association of University Professors was organized with John Dewey as the first president and Arthur Lovejoy as secretary. The idea of bringing the professors of America together for the consideration of questions of general interest, having been in the air for a number of years, finally took tangible form. Dewey delivered the keynote address in which he stressed the desirability of cooperation among scholars of the country for the study of the problems connected with instruction and research in higher education. As the *Nation* reported the news.

"The new association starts out under excellent auspices; it may fairly be expected to exert a wholesome influence on the further development of university life." [83] *

INTERPRETATION AND CONCLUSION

It is not strange that we have found non-conservative attitudes to the fore in this chapter, for non-conformists are most keenly aware of the pressures toward conformity. It is generally true that the less conservative elements in society are more concerned about the problem of social freedom. Those who essay to paddle upstream are more aware of the current than others drifting with it. Thus, it would be quite unwarranted to assume that the attitudes found in the periodicals represent those of college professors in general. Probably the majority of the profession are little concerned with the whole issue of academic freedom. One reason for such indifference may be readily understood when it is realized that only a few departments of a university deal with controversial social issues. Again, professors, like all other people, have been conditioned in their thinking by the values of the existent culture. Moreover, as we have pointed out, the faculty is likely to be subordinate to the administration.

"It is certainly one of the orthodox American's oldest but most firm illusions that a university is a hotbed of propaganda against all the worthwhile things of this life. . . . But, for the most part, American professors vote the straight Republican ticket, go to church regularly, believe in rugged individualism, abstain from cards and hard liquor, and otherwise lead pious and constructive lives." [84]

This opinion was expressed in 1932. Two years later we find the same opinion.

---

* It is to be regretted that the periodicals do not offer a more complete picture of professional organizations. Eight articles appeared after 1915, not including references to the Association that may be found in the discussions of specific cases of dismissal. All of these articles appeared in two magazines, the *Nation* and the *New Republic*. The author has decided that it is better to present nothing at all than these few data which are largely adversely critical. Nor do the periodicals discuss to any appreciable degree the college sections of the American Federation of Teachers.

For further information, consult *Educational Freedom and Democracy,* Second Yearbook of the John Dewey Society, D. Appleton-Century Co., 1938, Chapters 9 and 10.

"Anyone who is familiar with the genus in its native habitat must smile at the prevailing notion that the typical professor is a radical." [85]

Durkheim has developed at considerable length the sociological implications of the division of labor. He calls the solidarity resultant from division of labor "organic." The college or university is a complex whole exhibiting division of labor and the organic solidarity resultant therefrom. Academic specialization means that the process of education is interdependent and cooperative. On the other hand, there are various groups in the institution working at cross-purposes. Here is the president who must placate trustees and wealthy donors, real or potential; who seeks to preserve a harmonious relationship with the community and its institutions. Here are the professors, trained to follow intellectual ideals unhampered by external forces. The administration wishes to preserve the "good name" of the institution and to maintain smooth institutional efficiency. The professors, at least a portion of them, desire freedom to teach and investigate without interference.

Yet the problem ramifies far beyond the confines of these two groups. In order to understand the issues involved here, we must examine the very nature of society. In every society the *mores* and institutions are considered to be more or less beyond dispute. The values implicit in the culture of the present are always "right", sacred, and not to be criticized. The traditional ways are the "natural" ways and anything else violates human nature. The prevailing institutions require no justification, or at the most, are rationalized into dogmatic beliefs. The *status quo* tends to be upheld by all institutions, family, school, church, business and government. In each of these are vested interests which guard the *mores* by indoctrinating the young, controlling the organs of public opinion, and stamping out non-conformity. This is not to say, of course, that usages, *mores,* and institutions do not change nor that in periods of rapid social change with attendant disorganization the dominant values are not called into question by large numbers of people. We wish to emphasize, however, that society exists within a framework of social control and that, consequently, there is likely to be opposition to academic freedom at all times.

In the collegiate world the guardians of the *mores* are the legislatures (with all the pressure groups connected therewith), alumni, donors, vested interests in the community, trustees, presidents, and deans. Nor is the faculty unified and some may bring pressure, in the form of criticism, ridicule, and ostracism, upon the rash colleague who has "erred". Yet the attitudes of these groups are only precipitates of a community attitude. Thus we may conclude from the very nature of social organization that academic freedom is likely to be an ideal at all times. Some groups, to be sure, approach the ideal more closely than others. Certainly hundreds of professors in the social sciences in this country are thankful for an environment which tolerates a greater degree of freedom than do the regimented countries of the world. On the other hand, the preservation of the freedom which we possess requires constant vigilance, for there are at work, as indicated above, those forces which would defeat the democratic spirit.*

---

* During the years covered by this study there has been a wealth of material written about cases of dismissal. The figures participating in these dramas are professors both eminent arfd obscure. These cases have involved their professional careers and the welfare of their families, colleagues, indeed, the academic profession itself. Nevertheless the author has not attempted to present the innumerable facts and circumstances (even assuming that the periodicals published the "facts") surrounding each case. Such an attempt would run to many many pages.

REFERENCES

Academic Freedom

[1] *Scribner's,* XCIX, 115, 1936.
"What is Academic Freedom?", Gerald Chittenden.

[2] *Independent,* LXXI, 907, 1911.
"Trustees and Professors," Thaddeus P. Thomas.

[3] *Nation,* CXL, 293, 1935.
"Propaganda in the Schools."

[4] *Atlantic Monthly,* CXXI, 83, 1918.
"Freedom of the College," Alexander Meiklejohn.

[5] *Nation,* CXL, 449, 1935.
"On Academic Freedom," Joseph Krutch.

[6] *Atlantic Monthly,* CXIV, 1914.
"Academic Freedom," H. C. Warren.

[7] *Nation,* CII, 96, 1916.
"The Professor's Place in the World."

[8] *Nation,* XCVIII, 50, 1914.
"Free Speech and Professors."

[9] *Literary Digest,* XXV, 162, 1902.
"Sensationalism of College Professors."

[10] *Saturday Evening Post,* CCI, 32, 1929.
"Academic Vagaries."

[11] See No. 4.

[12] *Harper's,* CLXIX, 612, 1934.
"Forces that Control the Schools," Howard K. Beale.

[13] *New Republic,* XII, 328, 1917.
"Those Columbia Trustees," Randolph Bourne.

[14] *Literary Digest,* CXXX, 28, 1930.
"Sex Questionnaire and Academic Freedom."

[15] *New Republic,* LXXXIV, Sept. 25, 1935.
"Counter-attack at Pittsburgh," J. Alfred Wilner.

[16] *New Republic,* XLII, 57, 1925.
"Academic Freedom and Academic Tenure."

[17] *Forum,* XVII, 559, 1894.
"Research, the Vital Spirit of Teaching," G. Stanley Hall.

[18] *Atlantic Monthly,* CLVII, 236, 1936.
"Blind Alleys," Carl J. Friedrich.

[19] See No. 2.

[20] See No. 9.

[21] *New Republic,* LXXXII, 272, 1935.
"A Professor is Fired."

[22] *Atlantic Monthly,* CLV, 1935.
"Free Inquiry or Dogma?", James B. Conant.

[23] *World's Work*, XX, 13432, 1910.
"Are the Colleges Doing Their Job?", Arthur W. Page.
[24] *Literary Digest*, LI, 65, 1915.
"Is a College Professor A Hired Man?"
[25] *Forum*, L, 445, 1913.
"The Third American Sex," George C. Cook.
[26] *Atlantic Monthly*, XCVI, 790, 1905.
"Shall the University Become A Business Corporation," H. S. Pritchett.
[27] *New Republic*, LXXV, 149, 1933.
"Self-determination for Faculties," Harold Laski.
[28] *Scientific Monthly*, L, 1927.
"The Passing of the Professor," Otto Heller.
[29] *Independent*, CXII, 280, 1924.
"The Liberal College and Its Enemies," John Dewey.
[30] *New Republic*, XIII, 69, 1917.
"Academic Freedom," Arthur Livingston.
[31] *Nation*, CVI, 619, 1918.
"Trustees and Faculties," Academicus.
[32] See No. 25.
[33] See No. 29.
[34] *Nation*, CIV, 149, 1917.
"Academic Freedom."
[35] *Atlantic Monthly*, LXXXV, 488, 1900.
"Perplexities of a College President," One of the Guild.
[36] *New Republic*, XXVIII, 68, 1921.
"The Professor on Behalf of His Profession," J. E. Kirkpatrick.
[37] See No. 26.
[38] See-No. 29.
[39] *Harper's*, CLVIII, 391, 1929.
"The Academic Mind," Harold Laski.
[40] *Atlantic Monthly*, XCVII, 1906.
"The University President," Andrew S. Draper.
[41] See No. 31.
[42] *Harper's*, CLXIV, 314, 1932.
"The American College Presidents," Harold Laski.
[43] See No. 27.
[44] *Nation*, CXIII, 537, 1921.
"The Genus Professor," Max McConn.
[45] See No. 18.
[46] See No. 39.
[47] *Nation*, XCII, 397, 1911.
"Letter to the Editor."
[48] *Nation*, XCII, 518, 1911.
Editorial.

[49] *Nation,* CXVIII, 520, 1924.
Editorial.
[50] See No. 21.
[51] *Nation,* CI, Sup. 10, 1915.
"Effects on a University Faculty of Arbitrary Dismissals."
[52] *New Republic,* I, 18, 1915.
"Academic Freedom," Professor "Ordinarius."
[53] *Century,* XCII, 222, 1916.
"Academic Freedom," Vida Scudder.
[54] *Atlantic Monthly,* XCI, 152, 1903.
"Academic Freedom in Theory and in Practice," A. T. Hadley.
[55] *Century,* 208, June 1927.
"What does the University Think," Gerald W. Johnson.
[56] *New Republic,* XX, 312, 1920.
"Public Opinion in the Middle West."
[57] *Harper's,* CLIII, 144, 1926.
"The Pestiferous Alumni," Percy Marks.
[58] *Scribner's,* LXXII, 504, 1922.
"Another View of Alumni Control," Alumnus.
[59] *New Republic,* XIII, 69, 1917.
"Academic Freedom," Arthur Livingston.
[60] *Nation,* CXX, 369, 1925.
"The Life of a College Professor."
[61] *New Republic,* LXIV, 123, 1930.
"The Spoils System Enters College," John B. Hudson.
[62] *Harper's,* CLXX, 369, 1934.
"An Excuse for Universities," Gerald Johnson.
[63] *Nation,* CXII, 613, 1921.
"Teacher-baiting: The New Sport."
[64] *Forum,* LXXIV, 320, 1925.
"The Tennessee Evolution Law."
[65] *Literary Digest,* CX, July 11, 1931.
"Tennessee Sticks to Genesis."
[66] *Literary Digest,* CX, August 29, 1931.
"The Anti-Evolution Law," James Finney.
[67] *Literary Digest,* CXX, 39, 1935.
"The Clash Over Teachers' Oath Laws."
[68] *Saturday Evening Post,* CCVIII, 26, 1936.
"Legislating Patriotism."
[69] *Nation,* CXL, 13, 1935.
"In Support of the Constitution," Carl Becker.
[70] *Harper's,* CLXXII, 171, 1936.
"Teachers' Oaths," Carl Friedrich.
[71] *Nation,* CXLII, 437, 1936.

"Bombing Out the Middle Class."
[72] *Harper's,* CLXXV, 547, 1937.
"Professor's Freedom," Donald Slesinger.
[73] *Literary Digest,* XXVI, 918, 1903.
"Are American Professors 'Caged Employees'?"
[74] *Century,* CVI, 785, 1923.
"Educational Notes," Lawton Machall.
[75] See No. 4.
[76] *Nation,* CXXIII, 163, 1927.
"Must Colleges be Treadmills?"
[77] *Nation,* XCVIII, 50, 1914.
"Free Speech and Professors."
[78] *Nation,* CXXIV, 558, 1927.
"The Fight at West Chester."
[79] See No. 36.
[80] *Literary Digest,* XLIII, 1201, 1911.
"Rabbit-like Professors."
[81] *Forum,* L, 445, 1913.
"The Third American Sex," George Cook.
[82] *Forum,* LI, 321, 1914.
"The Professorial Quintain," F. B. R. Hellems.
[83] *Nation,* C, 146, 1915.
"Professors in Council."
[84] *American Mercury,* XXVIII, 207, 1932.
"Censorship Among the Learned," M. L. Radoff.
[85] See No. 62.

"I took occasion not long ago to ask a college dean who was the best teacher in his institution. He named a certain instructor.

'What is his rank?"

'Assistant Professor'.

'When will his appointment expire?'

'Shortly'.

"Will he be promoted?'

'No'.

'Why not?'

'He hasn't done anything!' "

ABRAHAM FLEXNER,
Atlantic Monthly, CIII, p. 840, 1909.

CHAPTER IV

Teaching and Research

INTRODUCTION

The most persistent problem of collegiate pedagogy, according to the periodicals, lies in the conflict between teaching and research. At the very beginning of the discussion, however, it may be well to point out that the college and the university are hardly comparable in respect to this problem. In the college there are only undergraduates while the university contains graduate departments of various kinds. Since devotion to scholarship is fundamental to the graduate schools of the university, the teachers there are expected to be engaged in some kind of productive scholarship. Without it their graduate courses and seminars are likely to suffer. Even apart from the teaching of graduate students, the professors of a university are engaged, and are encouraged to be engaged, in making contributions to knowledge, according to their training and talent. The university is an institution dedicated to the pursuit of truth and may be said to have social obligations that go beyond the group of students who constitute its enrollment at any one time. With the undergraduate schools, or colleges, the case is somewhat different. While some of the faculty members in colleges make contributions to the thought and knowledge of the times, their task is primarily undergraduate teaching.

There is another important different between the college and the university. The latter, due in part to its greater size, shows a more complex organization. Its fields of knowledge are more highly specialized. The members of the various departments of instruction easily come to take the view that they are teaching *subjects* instead of *students*. A man, for example, may be a member of the history department of a large university which includes ten instructors; but, in order to organize the instruction, each takes over certain special fields, such as American history since the Civil War, the French Revolution, etc. Such a specialist

123

is more obviously teaching subject-matter than the history instructor in the smaller college who is free to roam all over European history. With the greater division of labor in the university goes greater impersonality of relationships. The university teacher may lecture to large classes of students, very few of whom he knows even by name. The work of the university may be called urbanized education, for it stands in relation to the college as does the city to the village.*

DOES RESEARCH HAMPER TEACHING?

The majority of the articles analyzed in the pages which follow do not make this distinction, although some of them do. Possibly some of these critics would reply that, pedagogically, the trouble with the universities is that the graduate interest has almost swallowed up the interest in undergraduate teaching. At any rate, throughout the entire period covered by this study one finds protests against the intrusion of the research or scholarly interest upon teaching. "We seem to have fallen on a generation of few really great teachers," remarked the *World's Work* in 1901[1] and many have echoed the sentiment since that time. An ironical fact is pointed out in this connection.

"It is at least a curious coincidence that the development of the modern science of pedagogy, with its array of physiological and psychological data, should have been accompanied by a distinct decline in the prominence of the teacher."[2]

As we shall see later, some see no incompatibility between teaching and research but they are outnumbered. Even several of those who appear to disagree with the majority can be reconciled to it when we understand exactly what they mean. For instance, G. Stanley Hall wrote in 1894 that he considered research the "vital spirit of teaching" but he is careful to differentiate college and university professors, as the author has done, and tells us that he refers to the latter.[3] Seventeen years later it was said that a man cannot

---

* The distinction between the college and the university does not carry the implication that the latter is *better* than the former.

be the best teacher without creative work but it is added that "the mere mechanical compiling of uncorrelated facts, which makes up much so-called investigation, produces neither the true scholar nor the true teacher."[4]

Evidently, the periodical writers quoted see a real problem here. In its eccentric style *Time* classifies the members of the faculty.

"At most U. S. colleges there exist two kinds of faculty members: the teaching professors and the research professors. Dear to the heart of many an undergraduate is the teaching professor. Him they afterward remember for what little light and learning they possess. . . . But the research professors, who sometimes regard the civilizing of students as a vague, even faintly vulgar waste of time, are the darlings of their erudite colleagues and often of the president who feels the responsibility of keeping the university in good competitive position intellectually."[5]

Between the two groups, it adds, there is occasionally mild academic friction. Ten years ago an anonymous writer contributed an autobiographical account of the issue as it affected him personally: "A Letter from a Young Man who Found He did not Belong." Instead of going straight to the graduate school after completing his college course, he travelled and read extensively. Upon his return he was appointed an instructor in his alma mater. Not long after taking up his academic duties, he was approached about graduate work; but he rebelled at the idea and wrote popular articles instead. While he was given credit for a certain amount of originality in these, his colleagues did not consider them scholarly. Moreover, he liked teaching though most of his colleagues seemed to begrudge the time that it consumed. After being told definitely that the degree was a union card and that without it he could not advance professionally, he decided to quit.[6]

Perhaps the best statement of the difference in viewpoint between teaching and research is that of Abraham Flexner. He does not set up any hierarchy but feels that the two are separate and incompatible. The teaching attitude "disclaims at once the very disjunction that research presupposes. Its business is practical and human; pedagogic, not logical."[7] There is no conflict necessarily between the two interests, for "there is no issue between training minds and organizing facts." However, pedagogical vitality is just as valid in education as logical validity is in its domain. Teaching deals with "composite, living, organic combinations and wholes" while research is analytical and methodologically rigorous. The teacher should do research if he likes it; but, if not, he should seek other sources of relaxation and spiritual renewal. The investigator should teach if he desires; yet, in general, pedagogical duties are a hindrance and a waste of his energy. Another writer suggests that the two may be combined —up to a certain point.

"But in the effort to combine research and teaching, many a man who could have become a great teacher or a great investigator has fallen short of either distinction and become a mere commonplace failure at both. It is only once in a generation that an Agassiz appears who can achieve great success in both fields of work." [8]

Probably there have been numerous teachers who have been denied the full satisfactions of their classroom work by the pressure upon them to turn out publications; and, conversely, many research workers of high potentiality have worried along for years in a career taken up with the instruction of undergraduates in whom they were not interested.

One reason for the teaching-research dilemma is that most professors teach for a living, although their professional training has been along research lines. As early as 1895 we find reference to this dilemma.

"In the zeal for special research which . . . has become the ideal aim of most college instruction, it has come about that only the most brilliant scholars are chosen to be instructors, regardless of their lack of more strictly professional preparation and experience." [9]

In order to understand this inconsistency it is necessary to see how the professor is selected and trained. Regarding selection W. R. Castle writes as follows:

"Too often he is selected, not primarily, but exclusively, for his learning. A young man, after three or four years' devotion to his books, graduates from college *summa cum laude*. He knows few of his classmates because he has never had time to meet them. The book of college life he has never opened." [10]

The selection of bright scholars for the graduate school and, eventually, for the academic profession illustrates the self-perpetuating nature of social institutions. Those who make good grades and are well adjusted to the school environment may be attracted to an academic career. Such persons may resent criticism of the school system in the same way that the successful in economic life may resent criticism of the capitalistic *mores*. The success of each is bound up with the established institution and criticism of the institution is, in effect, a personal criticism. In short, the bright and diligent student who becomes a professor represents a vested interest.

The training in the graduate school alienates further the academic neophyte from the undergraduate. What is the nature of graduate work? Mr. Castle asserts that the attention is fixed upon minute research.

"After graduation he applies himself with even greater assiduity, deciphers obscure manuscripts, writes, a thesis on 'Boileau's Influence on Rousseau' . . . or on some rare genus of prehistoric mosquito, and then suddenly finds himself blinking in the face of an applauding world, a Doctor of Philosophy."

Other writers are equally outspoken in their adverse attitude toward the research leading to the doctorate. Mr. Allen, secretary of the Harvard Corporation (1926), refers to such theses as the feminine endings in the blank verse of various Elizabethan poets, and the position of the unemphatic object pronoun in Old French.

"Suppose I . . . set out to count all the bricks in the pavements of New York. You would at once call this piece of research futile. Why? Because it has no possible value to anyone. . . . Academic, brick-counting—that's what it is. . . . Professors want something definite, scientific, full of facts— small hard facts, with footnotes to back them up . . ." [11]

Yet, he adds, whenever he talks in this vein to his academic friends they leap upon him and label him Philistine.* A few

---

* For a vigorous criticism of research pursued in partial fulfillment of the requirements for the Ph. D., see Clarence C. Little, *The Awakening College*, op. cit., pp. 136-139.
"The almost unbelievable picayune fields of specialization that have come to be worshipped in this wholesale process of 'productiveness' can best be discovered by a perusal of the subjects of certain dissertations submitted as part of the requirement for the doctor of philosophy degree."

years ago the *Saturday Evening Post* published an article on the identical theme, written up as a conversation between a professor and a dean. The latter is telling that he is on his way to interview two candidates for a position at his school. Both are Phi Beta Kappa and both are well recommended by their respective graduate schools, Chicago and Columbia. Yet he is certain that neither represents what he wants. Even the better of the two will be infected with Ph. D.itis.

"He will be able, he will be zealous but he will be narrow in the range of his own interests and cheerfully contemptuous of interests not his own. His world will have been the world of the library; if he were in another department, it would have been the world of the laboratory; and he will quite honestly deny the truth of Stevenson's dictum that 'books are mighty bloodless substitutes for life.'"[12]

Shortly after Mr. Hutchins became president of the University of Chicago, he contributed an article to the *Review of Reviews* in which he put in a plea for, and promised some action on the problem of, training professors for a teaching career. Most doctors of philosophy, he asserts, never develop into productive scholars but are taken up with college teaching. Yet the training for the doctorate is almost uniformly a training in the acquisition of a research technique.

"The graduate schools of arts, literature, and science in the University of Chicago are in large part professional schools. They are producing teachers. A minority of their students become research workers. Yet the training for the doctorate in this country is almost uniformly training in the acquisition of a research technique, terminating in the preparation of a so-called original contribution to knowledge . . ."[13]

Yet most Ph. D.'s become teachers and not productive scholars— why, he does not know. Perhaps the rigorous discipline of the graduate school exhausts creative powers, perhaps most college professors are without creative powers in the first place, perhaps teaching schedules are too heavy. Probably all three of these possibilities suggested by President Hutchins contain some merit.

The attitude of a college teacher turned business man is quite vehement on the effect of the graduate school. He refers to the "stupendous doses" of learning administered there.

"Many a good man has been ruined by post-graduate work. Taken in moderation it is an excellent thing; but taken in the stupendous doses which are prescribed by our boards of trustees it is the most inhumanizing, fossilizing, dehydrating process known to man." [14]

This writer, it will be noted, places the blame upon the trustees. Certainly it is true that the administration cannot be held blameless, for it is in a position to promote effective teachers who do not possess the redoubtable doctoral degree. Yet the competitive process works against such a plan, each institution desiring to harbor an impressive array of doctors that can be printed in the college catalogue. Lest the attitude expressed above be considered merely the volatility of a disgruntled ex-professor, we may turn to a great scholar for corroboration. Many years ago G. Stanley Hall described the "dehydrating process" that constitutes part of the training of professors. He suggests a recipe for turning the freshness and spontaneity of youth "into the premature ripeness of age, eliminating the noon-day of consummate manhood": first you take a vigorous young man with rich emotions and a wholesome interest in the passing affairs and experiences of life.

"But in intellectual work he does not find companionship either warm or large. . . . At every point he is thrown back upon himself and pessimism with the Great Fatigue has touched him. . . . He has lost the flavor of conviction, and, if he has not positive ill-health, he is a moral valetudinarian." [15]

What effect does this emphasis upon research training and specialized scholarship have upon the process of teaching? What about the students? It is the verdict of the periodicals that they suffer. A large number of citations may be adduced on this point. Early in the century the *Forum* carried an account of the "Monastic Danger in Higher Education" whose author expressed the hope that those who are absorbed in their respective subjects to the exclusion of the undergraduate would retire to some congenial retreat "where the problems which absorb their energies would not be complicated by the existence of the undergraduate." [16] This, he claims, would be better for the college and the scholar. (But how is he to earn a living?). A few years later the *Nation* speaks with regret of the specialization on our college faculties. Such a condition obstructs mutual exchange of ideas among professors and has a decided effect upon the students who need a broad and deep culture rather than specialized knowledge.[17] Five years later (1913) the same journal published an article by a professor under the title, "Will the Worm Ever Turn?" in which the value of college teaching is lauded and the adverse effect of research upon teaching duly noted. Our classrooms are too often entrusted to men who are "impatient of detail, careless in presentation, full of their own mental processes, and unaware of those of their students."[18]

"It is a curious fact that as a rule a teacher gets a position on a college faculty not because he can teach, but by demonstrating that he has been taught." [19]

The newly hatched Ph. D. seeking a position may include among the items of self-advertisement a list of the distinguished scholars and scientists under whom he has studied, although these may have been poor or mediocre teachers themselves.

Some of these critics have no desire to ignore the value of the doctorate for research and for the instruction of graduate students.

"What is deplorable is that its possession should be held to entitle a man to a position as instructor in elementary courses. The ideal teacher certainly would be a scholar, but one fired with the enthusiasm to teach. . . . There are many such . . . but not enough to go round." [20]

Many of our doctors, it is said further, teach with meticulous accuracy but without enthusiasm. Some of these are even given responsibilities as student counsellors. This is a mistake. "He could give no advice concerning life because the freshman would know more of life than he."

Yes, agrees Professor George Boas, professors are ignorant. He objects to the past-time indulged in by certain academicians, namely, that of measuring in some more or less valid manner the ignorance of college students.

"What do teachers know? Do they know the human soul, or do they know facts, or do they know that there is such a thing as a problem of knowledge." [21]

Intimating that he has only recently returned from military service in the World War, he strikes out against the stupidity and futility of the higher learning. Subject-matter is deemed more important than students, who are sacrificed for what we think is scholarship. Men quite satisfactory as teachers are asked to resign because they do not belong to the "Ph. D.-ocracy"; while others with the degree will be employed at twice the salary, although with no guarantee that they can teach as well. He makes this observation:

"The pathos of such a sight never strikes a man within the university because he lacks the perspective; but when one returns after a year or two in other pursuits, such as the army, the university seems . . . a kingdom of shadows where ghosts teach living men."

Circumstances such as these, he concludes, go far to explain the evolution of the college student from the eager inquirer of the freshman year to the disillusioned senior.

The specialist assumes that his students will echo his enthusiasm for his little province of knowledge—certainly the best students. Every one who has been to college has probably had the misfortune to fall into the clutches of the professor who teaches the elementary course as though all of the class were about to embark on a professional career in the field. The students are confused and confounded, having been dropped suddenly into a strange world.

"Will not the real college teacher, on the other hand, remember that most of his students are never to follow the subject much further in the classroom and that the probability of their maintaining an interest in it on their own account will depend very largely on the degree to which they grasp it as a whole and the extent to which its relations are made plain to other parts of their experience and other subjects in the curriculum?" [22]

The identical theory of the relation of parts to whole in education was enunciated by Mr. Glenn Frank six years before he was elected president of the University of Wisconsin. He speaks of learning backward, not forward—backward, he seems to mean, from a logical, though not a psychological, point of view.

"We find ourselves interested in the whole of a subject and then undertake to find out something about its parts. Given that critical interest, learning is a quest we undertake upon our own initiative. The paradox of education is that you must grasp the whole before you acquire a genuine interest in the parts. It is this principle that is ignored in much college teaching." [23]

Latterly, this theory has been developed by *Gestalt* psychology. Yet the theory of the *Gestalt,* at least in its pedagogical implications, is not new to educational philosophers.

Apparently, minds of broad, synthetic scope are not common to the campus. They cannot teach their students in terms of wholes for the simple reason that they themselves have no grasp of the interrelatedness of knowledge. On this point Bernard DeVoto has written as follows:

"The historian saw no reason why psychology, anthropology, medicine, or any economics later than Adam Smith should intrude on history. The psychologist regarded logic as nonsense. The economist scorned literature, and the teacher of literature knew neither economics nor psychology, neither history nor medicine. Try to bring one science to bear on another, and you were snubbed. All were ignorant of, or indifferent to, all subjects but their own . . . " [24]

On this point we find agreement from one who probably has had more influence upon American education than any other living man. Dewey, writing in the *Independent* (1924), asserts that an excess of specialization militates against a liberal education.

"Specialism is the vogue of the day in scholarship. While some degree of specialism is indispensable, in excess it contributes to a decline of liberality of mind." [25] *

From all that has been said, it seems clear that the periodicals are in substantial agreement on this matter. Devotion to research and scholarship, though not necessarily unworthy, is a hindrance to the development and maintenance of effective teaching. There are exceptions to be sure, but they alter the principle in no significant way.†

---

* How many college professors could be called educated by Milton's definition: "I call, therefore, a complete and generous education that which fits a man to perform justly, skilfully, and magnanimously all the offices, both private and public, of peace and war." *Tractate on Education,* 1644.

† A few years ago (1933) the A.A.U.P. published a report by the committee on college and university teaching. One major item considered was the relation of teaching to research. The idea of their mutually obstructive influences was brought out quite definitely, although it is further asserted that the two activities "are by no means inharmonious." *College and University Teaching,* A.A.U.P., 1933, pp. 21-22, 53-56.

See also Paul Klapper (ed.) *College Teaching,* World Book Co., 1920, Chapter 2. Here is presented a plan for the professional training of college teachers.

Is Research Worth While?

As a matter of fact, not all of the magazines admit that the research work accomplished at the sacrifice of the students is valuable. At the beginning of the century a writer in *Forum* poked fun at one brand of scholarship by describing one professor who is said to "know more about fen-drainage in the thirteenth century than any other living person except one dreadfully old man in Germany who is beginning to forget about it."[26] Dean McConn of Lehigh University has upon several occasions referred with disparagement to that which passes for productive scholarship. He classifies the "Genus Professor" into four categories, number two being "Professor Germanicus."

"By the German professor I mean the laborious, exhaustive investigator of some narrowly circumscribed specialty—the Latin vocative, for example, the feeding habits of the bedbug, the jawbone of the ass. . . . The primary indication for the determination of this species is a total indifference to any question of practical utility in connection with his field of study. . . . When once a young professor had seen his name in print, you could predict with confidence that he would belong to the new species. . . . He would become a mere machine for the alternate production and consumption of the contents of the journals . . ."[27]

He claims that this species is the most abundant of all in our universities and is likely to be the only extant variety of the genus professor very soon "since its special food supply is still on the increase." Eight years later (1929) he asks the question, "When is a Teacher not a Teacher." First, the point is made that the research and teaching viewpoints are different and even inimical to each other. College teachers "know their stuff," the students concede, but they cannot teach. But, he asks, does the existing system promote research?

"I wonder if more than one-tenth of the army of college teachers now 'producing' under compulsion produce anything of substantial value. For most of them research is also routine. Their little papers clutter up our learned journals. . . . I suspect that most of them are camp-followers in the army against ignorance, intent, not on the campaign, but on the commissary."[28]

President James B. Conant of Harvard has stated that one serious charge brought against modern scholarship is that it is trivial. He likens a certain type of research to stamp-collecting—fascinating for those who like it but hardly of any palpable social importance.

"I think any candid observer will admit that a fair proportion of present-day research is trivial, but no one regrets this more than the scholars themselves. However fascinating stamp-collecting may be as an avocation, no one would suppose that it should be a university subject, and the line between stamp-collecting and certain types of research is admittedly very thin."[29]

However, he warns that we must beware of curbing activities which may lead to important findings.

But we need not confine ourselves to the attitudes expressed by deans and presidents. Professors have confessed to doubts concerning the value of the highly specialized scholarship in which they are engaged. One of these, a self-styled pedagogue in revolt, admits that there is a loss of a sense of proportion in the work he is carrying on in connection with his seminar. Both pedagogue and student must labor under a load of heavy tomes in order to fulfill the demands of contemporary academic demands.

"Month by month and week by week they multiply, tomes, articles, pages upon pages upon the reading of a word or phrase, discussion after discussion upon some minute point of fact . . . discussions often inspired less by passion for truth than by the bitter joy of proving that some other scholar, in a rival university, is in the wrong." [30] *

The prize confession in this respect is one written by an eminent classical scholar over twenty-five years ago. He personifies his mental conflict by giving names to the two tendencies struggling for dominance of his personality: Mr. Homo and Dr. Scholarship. Having published a doctoral thesis five years before on the Sundry Suffixes in S, he is now in the throes of producing a book on the Consonantal Terminations in the Comedies of Terence. But Mr. Homo, long in subjection, is asserting himself in a most annoying manner and the work is not moving along as smoothly as it should. In the writer's fantasy of conflict Mr. Homo—the uninstitutional-

---

* It is interesting to observe that most of the research subjects singled out for criticism by the periodicals are in the field of language and literature. Yet Flexner speaks of social science research in words of unmistakable disparagement. Flexner, op. cit., p. 127.

ized person—is badgering Dr. Scholarship for his solemn ways and his trivial work. He forces the latter to admit that the students are not interested, nor should they be. The people at large are certainly not interested in nor edified by studies in Consonantal Terminations. Who then? "The scholars of the country" replies Dr. Scholarship with pride. In answer to Mr. Homo's next question concerning the number of scholars in the country who are likely to read the proposed study, the learned doctor is compelled to admit that there are very few, possibly a dozen. Thereupon the irrepressible Mr. Homo, the part of the man that has never been conditioned to professorial scholarship, launches into a tirade against the whole system that robs a man of physical, intellectual, and spiritual growth, cheats his classes, and in general confuses means and ends. Waste, waste, absolute waste, cries Mr. Homo.

"I am objecting to the sham of writing merely for the sake of writing and the pretense of scholarship for the sake of gratifying personal vanity, receiving calls to coveted positions, or ministering to the greed of book concerns." [31]

Mr. Homo does not go to the extreme of suggesting that Dr. Scholarship will never have anything to contribute to the knowledge of the world. He does believe nevertheless that at the age of thirty it is rather presumptuous for the doctor to expect to have anything of real merit to contribute.

Yet the periodicals do not categorically condemn academic research and scholarship. Professor A. N. Whitehead, the philosopher, considers it a great mistake to estimate the value of each member of the faculty by the printed work signed with his name. Nevertheless,

". . . when all allowances have been made, one good test for the general efficiency of a faculty is that as a whole it shall be producing in published form its quota of contributions to thought. Such a quota is to be estimated in weight of thought, and not by the number of words." [33]

An earlier writer alleges that the best teachers "are not only great teachers, but philosophers, poets, writers, scientific investigators." He merely objects to that type of research which represents the piling up of uncorrelated data.[34] Professor Michael Pupin has written of "Pioneering Professors" who have led the way in the achievements of modern science. Newton was a professor and so was Volta, Oersted, and Faraday. University professors still remain the pioneers of electrical science and the same is true in many other fields. This is a fitting answer, he asserts, to the claim that the professor of science is an apostle of abstract theories that contribute little to the solution of practical problems. Far from being vacuous theorists they have furnished "the blood and brains with which the practical man has worked."[35]

Provost Josiah H. Penniman of the University of Pennsylvania refers to the service rendered by university research. The physical sciences and psychology perform services for many types of industries through their industrial research departments. No less a person than Benjamin Franklin said that there was no incompatibility between culture and applied knowledge.

"Universities have not stood still. They have kept pace with the progress of civilization. Especially in the last few years they have shown amazing ability to adjust themselves to the life all about them. There is scarcely an activity of any consequence to which universities are not addressing themselves and concerning which they are not consulted." [36]

More abstract but of the same attitude is that expressed by President Conant. After criticizing much research as trivial he turns to the other side of the ledger and describes the academic community at its best.

"At their best academic communities have been composed of men living consecrated lives—lives devoted to the passionate but almost selfless search for the truth. Such men have profoundly influenced the students and the world at large; they are honored and reverenced for their sincerity and their unswerving attachment to an ideal." [37]

He is convinced that it would be a serious mistake for our colleges and universities to stop investigating and devote themselves solely to teaching and assimilating what we know.*

---

* The A.A.U.P. committee report on teaching (op. cit.) cites the attitude of a college president that is less favorable to research than that of Harvard's president. Upon being presented with a complimentary copy of a book written by one of the faculty, he observed that, if the professor had time to write a book, he had time for more teaching at the college!

TEACHING MAY HAMPER RESEARCH

Research hampers teaching but the converse may be equally true. One difficulty with the progress of productive scholarship is that scholars are burdened too much with teaching duties. It is a shame, says an early writer in the *Forum,* to shackle the creative individuality of the genuine scholar with routine, lesson-hearing duties. While it is important to exert a moral influence over the undergraduate, this result is achieved at a sacrifice of the mental powers of the faculty. "Excessive teaching palls and kills" the research spirit.[38] The *Nation* agrees that the remedy for the lack of encouragement to original investigation is to reduce the teaching hours of potential contributors to knowledge—and relieve them of the miscellaneous committee work that ordinarily falls to the lot of the American professor. This is easier to say than to apply in actual practice, however.

"It is not wholly easy to recognize the investigator who is worthy of this special exemption. The greater part of university professors are not notable investigators but find their largest usefulness precisely in their teaching and in their administrative activities." [39]

Yet it is said that a certain amount of teaching is good for scholarly specialists. Teaching is a "clarifying work" and brings the scholar into ordinary human relations. Again we quote Professor White-head:

"Do you want your researchers to be imaginative? Then bring them into intellectual sympathy with the young at the most eager, imaginative period of life, when intellects are just entering upon their mature discipline."

As suggested in the chapter dealing with personality, teaching easily dulls the mental processes of the professor. The repetition of the same ideas year after year to groups of immature students is hardly favorable to the flowering of creative thought. The man of originality needs freedom to collect his data and work out his interpretations but the institutionalized learning of the school is not favorable to such originality, either for teachers or for students. Under the impact of classroom duties all but the most robust intellects are likely to get into a rut. Ideas become stereotyped through repetition, hypotheses become doctrines; in other words, the creative thinker and investigator become mere pedagogues. Moreover, because of the exigencies of the marking system, the tendency is to emphasize tangible and formal facts whereas vital **problems are more elusive.** Briefly expressed, institutionalization hampers the creative powers of the scholar and scientist.*

The character of our teaching must be included among the forces making for the triumph of mediocrity in scholarship. We try to teach too much, spoon-feeding our students instead of throwing them upon their own resources.[40] Professor Munsterberg, the psychologist, contributed an article to the *Atlantic Monthly* on the status of productive scholarship in America in which he manifests a dubious regard for teaching ability. In six weeks, he asserts, anyone with a forcible way of presentation and an average intellect can become a fine teacher—of any subject. This is certainly a striking statement but Munsterberg justifies himself.

"The student cannot judge whether the thoughts brought forward in the lecture are the instructor's own thoughts, or a rehash of the contents of half a dozen text-books; or even if they are his own thoughts, whether they have any legs to stand on." [41]

Both of these writers, in analyzing the hindrances to the progress of productive scholarship, go beyond the factor of excessive teaching loads. With sociological insight they refer to factors of which the teaching load is merely symptomatic. Both agree that in America scholarship needs more social recognition and prestige so that better men are attracted. The first writer adds:

"A strong force making difficult first rate work is the lack of repose that characterizes our people. . . . Perhaps it is true that too many of our universities are in, or near, great cities which present too many distractions— social and political."

It appears true in the realm of science and scholarship as in art that nothing of lasting value can be created in haste. Without much question our technological progress and the rich commercial possibilities of a new country have played their parts in fostering an American spirit that is superficial and hurried.

---

* "The effect of formalism upon personality is to starve its higher life . . ." C. H. Cooley, *Social Organization,* Scribner's, 1909, p. 343.

What Can Be Done?

Why is the professor interested in research? There are many reasons, of course. Intellectual curiosity constitutes one motive, a genuine interest, that is, in advancing one's knowledge in a specialized field of study. The desire for recognition is also important in any general interpretation. Aside from these, there is the economic motive and it is this factor that is discussed most fully in the periodicals. It is said that good teaching is not rewarded while research and publications give status and aid in the securing of a better position or in obtaining an increase in salary. Two deans suggest independently that the universities make definite provision for attaching economic reward to good teaching. "Why", asks one, "promote teachers almost exclusively on the basis of their success as investigators? Why not appraise good teaching as such and give it its due reward in rank and salary?"[42] The other recommends that every institution provide for two to ten "super-professorships" carrying at least one thousand dollars excess on the salary scale for men pre-eminent as teachers. Further, in employing new instructors, administrators and department heads should take as much cognizance of a man's teaching power as the publicity value of his research-writing to the institution.[43] Both of these men call deplorable the attitude, found among some research men, that the university would be a fine place if it were not for the students.

In every group the majority are likely to accept those values current at the time. Such acceptance, sociologically, is essential to social adjustment. The academic group is a case in point, for if the rewards for research publication predominate over those for teaching, it is natural that professors will be guided into the former field, particularly in a commercial culture. Certainly it is within the power of the trustees and presidents of our colleges and universities to stimulate good teaching by paying extraordinary salaries for teaching services of a high calibre.

"Presidents protest that the exceptional undergraduate teacher is as precious to them as the exceptional researcher; but they open their purse strings to the investigator." [44]

This situation goes far to account for the advice given to younger professors by those inured to the system.

"A few years ago an acquaintance disclosed to me that the only sure road to academic preferment was to publish. 'Publish what?' said I innocently. 'Pages, no matter what,' said he in a whisper, with a glance to see that no one could overhear." [45]

Yet good teaching is not so easily detected. The fruits of the learning process are intangible. This fact has already been referred to in connection with the expenditure of university funds, for the governors are said to be desirous of investing the money available in places where it will show. Will it satisfy them to state that money invested in good teaching will show up, in the long run, in the personalities of the graduates? A number of writers, most of them teachers, point out this intangibility.

"The teacher realizes that he need not look for the fruit of his teaching in the undergraduate but in the middle-aged man." [46]

It is also said that this intangibility is not so prominent in other occupations. The business man cannot see why anyone should want to pursue a vocation the results of which are so impalpable.

"A physician cures diseases and makes money; even a clergyman, although he makes little money, secures conversions and fills churches; but what, what does a college professor do?" [47]

Professor Whitehead defines the proper function of a university as the "imaginative acquisition of knowledge" but hastens to add that imagination cannot be measured by the yard, or weighed by the pound.[48] Similarly, Professor Canby, the well-known teacher of English, admits that "good teaching is elusive, subject to false testimony, slow in its effects, hard to estimate, requiring time and trouble to search out."[49]

Conclusion

The material of this chapter is analyzed in Chapter 6 but a few points of interpretation may be suggested here. As in the previous chapters, we find protests against the existing order of things— in this case, against the emphasis upon specialized scholarship and research. These protests come closer to the academic *mores* than any other criticisms of the profession found in this study. Moreover, a great many of these protests have been written by professors. Here is heresy that cannot be ignored by the group. The professor may find fault with the conduct of business and government, the activities of the church, or with the social system in general; and, though many of his colleagues will disapprove, others will heartily affirm his attitude. But how many have the audacity to disparage the *mores* of the academicians themselves? In the academic group, as in every group, loyalty is expected of the constituent members. Whenever deviation from group standards occurs, the means of control well-known to the student of group life begin to operate: persuasion, ostracism, ridicule, labels, and all the rest. The group tries to dissuade the non-conformist by calling his activities and utterances "foolish" and "misguided". Some look askance and avoid one who is "queer", while others with brilliant analyses show how ridiculous are the ideas of the errant one. He is branded a traitor to the academic cause, a fanatic, a nuisance. Indeed, the most persistent persecution may come from those who, having inhibited their rebellious impulses, nevertheless are troubled by the uneasy feeling that the critic is right after all.

REFERENCES

TEACHING AND RESEARCH

[1] *World's Work,* III, 1901.
   "About the Overproduction of Scholars."
[2] *Nation,* LXX, 1900.
   "The Decline of Teaching."
[3] *Forum,* XVII, 559, 1894.
   "Research, the Vital Spirit of Teaching," G. S. Hall.
[4] *Literary Digest,* XLIII, 356, 1911.
   "Exalting the Teacher's Trade."
[5] *Time,* XIV, 27, 1929.
   "Teacher Snubbed."
[6] *Century,* CXVI, 544, 1926.
   "A Letter from a Young Man Who Found He Did Not Belong."
[7] *Atlantic Monthly,* CIII, 840, 1909.
   "The Problem of College Pedagogy," Abraham Flexner.

[8] *World's Work*, III, 913, 1901.
   "For Better Teaching and Research."
[9] *Review of Reviews*, XI, 217, 1895.
   "Needed Reforms in College Teaching."
[10] *Atlantic Monthly*, CIV, 554, 1909.
   "The College and the Freshmen," W. R. Castle.
[11] *Independent*, CXVI, 411, 1926.
   "The Fetish of the Ph. D.," Frederick L. Allen.
[12] *Saturday Evening Post*, CCIV, 55, 1932.
   "Practice what you Teach," James W. Linn.
[13] *Review of Reviews*, LXXXI, 99, 1930.
   "Training Professors and Paying Them," Robert M. Hutchins.
[14] *Outlook*, CXXIX, 645, 1921.
   "Why I Gave Up Teaching for Business," Kenneth Groesbeck.
[15] *Forum*, XVII, 1894.
   "Scholarship in the Training of Professors," G. S. Hall.
[16] *Forum*, XXXII, 244, 1901.
   "The Monastic Danger in Higher Education," H. W. Horwill.
[17] *Nation*, LXXXVI, 277, 1908.
   "Specialized College Faculty."
[18] *Nation*, XCVI, 1913.
   "Will the Worm Ever Turn?"
[19] *World's Work*, XX, 13432, 1910.
   "Are the Colleges Doing Their Job?" Arthur W. Page.
[20] See No. 10.
[21] *Atlantic Monthly*, CXXVII, 668, 1921.
   "What do Teacher's Know?" George Boas.
[22] *Century*, LXXXVIII, 51, 1914.
   "What is Wrong with the College?" H. C. Goddard.
[23] *Century*, XCVIII, 651, 1919.
   "Learning Backward Instead of Forward," Glenn Frank.
[24] *Harper's*, CLIV, 253, 1926.
   "College and the Exceptional Man," Bernard DeVoto.
[25] *Independent*, CXII, 280, 1924.
   "The Liberal College and Its Enemies," John Dewey.
[26] See No. 16.
[27] *Nation*, CXIII, 537, 1921.
   "The Genus Professor," Max McConn.
[28] *North American Review*, CCXXVIII, 410, 1929.
   "When Is a Teacher Not a Teacher?" Max McConn
[29] *Atlantic Monthly*, CLV, 1935.
   "Free Inquiry or Dogma," James B. Conant.
[30] *Atlantic Monthly*, CXLII, 353, 1928.
   "The Pedagogue in Revolt."

[31] *Atlantic Monthly,* CIV, 611, 1909.
"The Making of a Professor," Grant Showerman.
[32] *Atlantic Monthly,* CLVII, 236, 1936.
"Blind Alleys," Carl Friedrich.
[33] *Atlantic Monthly,* CXLI, 638, 1928.
"Universities and their Function," A. N. Whitehead.
[34] See No. 4.
[35] *Literary Digest,* C, 74, 1929.
"Our Debt to the Professor."
[36] *World's Work,* CLII, 193, 1926.
"Universities as Public Service Corporations," Josiah H. Penniman.
[37] See No. 29.
[38] See No. 3.
[39] *Nation,* LXXIV, 136, 1902.
"Investigator as Teacher."
[40] *Atlantic Monthly,* CVIII, 1911.
"Darwin at an American University," P. C. Maclaurin.
[41] *Atlantic Monthly,* LXXXVIII, 615, 1901.
"Productive Scholarship in America," Hugo Munsterberg.
[42] See No. 28.
[43] *Outlook,* 1928.
"Our Truant Professors," A. Hibbard.
[44] *Nation,* XCIV, 52, 1912.
"Personality and the Professor."
[45] *Atlantic Monthly,* 1913.
"A Confession of One Behind the Times."
[46] *Literary Digest,* L, 1020, 1915.
"Professorial Flaws Seen by the Student," Brooks Shepard.
[47] *Atlantic Monthly,* CXXI, 218, 1918.
"Why Teach?" Robert M. Gay.
[48] See No. 33.
[49] *Harper's,* CXXVI, 782, 1912.
"The Professor," Henry S. Canby.

Verily, verily, I say unto you,
The professor's is an unhappy lot:
His it is to be damned if he do,
As damned he was when he did not.
—*Atlantic Monthly,* July, 1933.

CHAPTER V

The Professor in Political Affairs

With few exceptions, the periodical discussion of the political activities of American professors centers about two events, the War and the New Deal. This does not signify, of course, that college professors have taken no part in local, state, and national politics except during these two periods. Indeed, one could contribute greatly to our knowledge of the academic profession by investigating the extent of its political and community participation. It is only at certain periods that his participation becomes of sufficient popular interest to win the attention of the magazine editors but the less sensational activities of many professors in guiding the practical affairs of the nation constitute a long and, as yet, unwritten chapter.

The War

Hardly was war declared when the *New Republic* referred to the influence of the academicians in effecting American participation.

"If the several important professional and social groups could have voted separately on the question of war and peace, the list of college professors would probably have yielded the largest majority in favor of war, except perhaps that contained in the Social Register."[1]

Magazine and newspaper writers were said to have been of the same attitude, popularizing what the professors had been thinking. The latter, headed by President Wilson who had been a professor himself, "contributed more effectively to the decision in favor of war than did the farmers, the business men, or the politicians." C. Hartley Grattan, writing in the *American Mercury* in 1927, tells how "The Historians Cut Loose" as early as 1914. By the end of July of the latter year the professors were "restive and fuming" and by the end of August they were "in violent eruption."

"Thereafter, for five long years, the word objectivity was abolished from their vocabularies. They harangued Kiwanis, they wrote letters to the newspapers, they preached in churches, they invaded the movie-parlors, they roared like lions. And in 1917 they submitted themselves eagerly and almost unanimously to the high uses of the Creel Press Bureau." [2]

Relatively few of the "blood-sweating" historians, he says further, operated independently. Most of them were enlisted by one or another of the "current spy-hunting and Hun-chewing societies." The writing of the pamphlets published by the Creel Bureau was largely done by the "embattled historians." The first one of these, entitled "How the War Came to America," was circulated to the extent of over five million copies. At one time Mr. Creel boasted that no less than twenty-five hundred historians were on his list while others went to work for other patriotic agencies.*

Of course, the historians were not unique in this respect. Charles Angoff tells more concerning the higher learning and the war. Statement after statement is quoted to show the belligerence of academicians before 1917. A professor of philosophy wrote to a colleague in London:

"'I should be a poor professor of philosophy, and in particular of moral philosophy, if I left my classes in the least doubt as to how to view such things.'"

By May, 1916, he was saying:

"We believe that the fabric of civilization embodied in free government and diversity of nationality, is menaced by Teutonic aggression, and that the foundations of public right are endangered by the violation of Belgium and the atrocities of the submarine war. We are convinced that our political ideals and our national safety are bound up with the cause of the Allies, and that their defeat would mean moral and material disaster to our country."

This pronouncement became one of the principles of a Citizen's League for America and the Allies formed in Boston at that time.

A historian composed a book in 1916 entitled, "Germany versus Civilization." Of this learned analysis, Mr. Angoff says:

"He found by a close process of reasoning that the German was nothing but a modern Hun, showing all his ancestors' abominable vices: unrestrained drinking, open dissoluteness, barbarity, mendacity, and so on. . . . Wagner's music reflected 'the unrestrained passions of war, lust and cunning that

---

* Additional facts are given in George Creel, *How We Advertised America,* Harper's, 1920, especially Chapter viii.

belong to an uncivilized race.' . . . The general opinion that Germany had once been the home of science and philosophy was shown to be altogether mistaken."

Similarly, a social psychologist published "American Neutrality, its Cause and Cure" in 1916. In it he asserted that our country was blind to its great opportunities for Service but that everything would turn out well in the end when the United States joined the Allies.

In January, 1917, there was founded the "National Defense and International Digest," a magazine devoted to the awakening of moral idealism with particular reference to the war in progress on the other side of the Atlantic. In one of its first issues, a well-known sociologist pontificated:

" 'The world situation today is the most critical one in human history, and some of our pacifists are doing their best to put civilization back a thousand years. . . . There is only one issue out of this war that can bring world peace, and that is the surrender of the Central Powers to the Allied Powers —surrender as complete as that of Great Britain to the American Colonies.' "

The United States, at that time, had not yet entered the war, Mr. Angoff points out, but these proclamations by the learned were already having an effect in the colleges. Persons holding pacifist views or opinions unfriendly to any of the Allies were forbidden the lecture rooms of the colleges. On February 10, 1917, Count Ilya Tolstoy was scheduled to speak at Columbia on the life of his father, Count Leo Tolstoy, who preached Christian love, but at the last minute the authorities refused to allow it.

But "all the high doings of the academic soldiers of civilization in 1915 and 1916 were merely practice work compared with their heroic deeds after the United States declared war on the Central Powers." In a strongly ironical vein Angoff refers to the "big-hearted and high-minded way in which they laid their intellectual gifts upon the altar of the nation." Two professors were the intellectual mainstays of the National Security League. They amassed a tremendous amount of "authentic" historical data proving conclusively that Germany was the enemy of everything in civilization. Another sociologist, who secured much of his graduate training in Germany, gave utterance to his hostility with prayerful earnestness:

> " 'This will be an intolerable world until the Germans have once and for-ever recanted, with all it involves, that most hellish heresy that has ever menaced civilization: There is no God, but power and Prussia is its prophet. . . . Now is our Gethsemane.' " [3]

Propaganda was not the only field of academic service. Research and scholarship had many fields of application in those days. Professors worked out the system of intelligence tests, compounded poisonous gases and devised gas masks, organized schools for the training of fliers, and invented codes for the communication of military secrets. Other professors plotted the commerce of the world, studied Germany closely, mobilized the youth of the country, converting colleges into army camps. The separate listing of professorial activities would be an almost interminable task.

> "There have been captains, majors, colonels, and even brigadier-generals whose incoming mail, addressed to Professor——, or Dr.——, or Dean——, has betrayed to unsuspecting clerks the late herbivorous habits of these sons of Mars. The khaki has been worn by many a knight of learning, who had never met any crisis but a crucial experiment, or handled any weapon but a pen, or faced any foe but a hostile audience. . . . The professor has been having the time of his life." [4]

Even before the Armistice was signed the president of the University of Wisconsin had described the war activities of his university, faculty and students, in the *Review of Reviews*. We may take his account as an example, not typical in all probability but nevertheless illuminating, of the war work of faculties. Leaves of absence were granted by the regents for those performing public service for national defense. By June, 1918, one hundred and eighty-seven members of the faculty were on leave. Of these one hundred and twenty-six were in the army, eleven in the navy, ten in the Red Cross, and forty in civilian service. The war work of the Wisconsin faculty was of several different kinds. Within the university new courses were introduced to fit students for special services. Such courses included aeronautics, bacteriology, French, geology, history, home economics, horticulture, military science, political science, and wireless telegraphy. Vocational training was offered to gunsmiths, machinists, electricians, and blacksmiths. In regard to research there were numerous contributions such as the work on gas defense and submarine detection. Concerning the first, fifteen members of the faculty devoted their energies to the study of methods of manufacture in quantity, the physiological effects and the remedies, and gas mask protection.

"In conclusion it may be said that the faculty and students have not only been willing but eager to participate in war work. Probably never since the days of the Civil War has there been so united a spirit. The early recogni- tion of the fundamental principles involved in the world contest has made each one feel the imperative necessity of making some contribution, how- ever small, toward overthrowing the evil plans of Germany and thus making possible the continuance in the world of a moral civilization." [5]

All the universities were willing to help. Mr. Robert L. Kelley, executive secretary of the council of church boards of education in the United States, presented some statistics in *Scribner's,* January, 1918. Princeton sent forty of its faculty into war service, fifty went from the University of Chicago, fifty from North- western, University of Louisville, and Colorado, forty from Yale, and seventy-five from Wisconsin. These are only a few of a long list of institutions "which cheerfully released their best professors and reorganized departments wholesale." With such stirring activi- ties of the faculty before them, one can readily imagine "the pulsing patriotism of the students now in school." No more do we see the bespectacled, bewhiskered type of professor stumbling about the campus but keen, alert young men with high ability and tech- nical training eager to do their bit for their country.

"If this is a war between the German schoolmaster and the American schoolmaster, as has been said, we are indeed willing to commit with con- fidence the leadership of our cause to those who have had the training afforded by that most unique institution, the American college, and to pay again a tribute of respect to that pervading influence of higher education which for two and one-half centuries has quietly but persistently leavened our population with the very essence of Americanism in ideal and training." [6]

Mr. Kelley concludes that "there still seems to be plenty of red blood in the typical college faculty." (Of course, he has his own definition of "red blood." Shall we consider those who actively opposed American participation red-blooded or merely foolhardy and treasonable? Attitudes have a way of affecting terminology.)

The role played by men of the academic profession has been one of the minor surprises of the war, according to a professor who served as a captain in the army. Reviewing the portion of the academician in the international holocaust shortly after the cessation of hostilities, Gordon H. Gerould refers to various countries where the services of college faculties had been conspicuous. "Even in Germany professors were conspicuous, though what they did and said brought no glory to learning and was an affront to the guild of pedagogues." The efficiency of these men in war-time has refuted thoroughly the "ancient libellous assumption that they constituted an absent-minded third sex." Many entered the fighting ranks while others were numbered among the staffs of the Military Intelligence Division, the Chemical Warfare Service, the War Industries Board, the Ordnance department, the Red Cross, the Division of Military Aeronautics, and the War Research Council.

> "The professor has done a remarkably large number of different things and has done most of them successfully. He has proved himself a leader and executive as well as an investigator which is precisely where the element of surprise comes in." [7]

Several years later, Arthur T. Hadley, president-emeritus of Yale University, agrees that the professors in war-time service "almost always did extremely well."[8]

On the other hand, the writers in the *American Mercury* mentioned above, are distinctly less complimentary. Mr. Grattan considers the "grossly biased text-books" of the patriotic historians bad enough but the world was to suffer something far worse.

> "The historians . . . were ordered in great swarms to Paris and so got their fingers into the pie of Versailles. . . . Some of the most vicious and imbecilic schemes adopted at Versailles . . . are primarily attributable to the influence exerted by American professors serving the House commission . . ."

What effects did the war have upon the profession? Mr. Gerould asserts that the professor discovered during the war that the "wide, wide world was not so different from his own world, after all, and was in no wise terrifying." Army conferences, for example, were not very different from academic committee meetings. He has developed a changed attitude toward various sorts of practical men and ought to be a better teacher for the discovery of the fallibilities of non-academic men.

"The rank and file of capable business men and lawyers and engineers are not so formidable in their practical wisdom as they are reputed to be. Flung out of their proper orbits, they show their traditional energy, to be sure, but they exhibit also certain failings that have been little dwelt upon. They prove to be rather careless creatures, not gifted with imagination, and not particularly notable for their power to attack new lines of work. . . . The professor has shown himself to be quite as good a man as any of them."

As a result of their war experience, professors should be less impressed with the prestige of the trustees, though more sympathetic with their ofttimes fumbling attempts to advance the cause of education.

A writer in the *Atlantic Monthly* hopes that the "Demobilized Professor" will carry back to the classroom the vital, creative spirit which animated his kind during the critical days of '17 and '18. During the war the success of academic men in service was stimulated by the bait of a live and urgent problem. Can such bait be held out to the students now?

"Here then is a new outlook and opportunity for American colleges to confirm and to exploit the new public interest; to reanimate all humane studies by connecting them with the enlivened humanity of the American youth; to focus the attention of students on the great outstanding problems . . . to create in every student the feeling that these problems are his problems. . . . To enter upon this new enterprise together will continue the fine comradeships of war, and will convert into powerful agencies of constructive peace the memories of the great days spent in the shadow of world-wide calamity." [9]

By the way of interpretation the author would like to make two comments. In the first place, one can understand well enough the alacrity with which academic men threw themselves into war work. Their intellectual duties tend to be rather anemic at times and their nerves and muscles cry out for action. The war comes and with it opportunities to escape from the thin realities of the intellectual life.* Perhaps this eagerness for action helps to account for the extremely zealous patriotism displayed by certain of their number on the platform and in books and pamphlets. Ideals of science and scholarship might suffer but what are these beside the satisfaction of frustrated emotions? Life, full and vigorous, beckoned; let intellectual ideals be hanged. Perhaps political causes of the present day possess the same appeal to certain academicians in their respective countries. For such men devotion to a cause may give a sense of freedom that scholarship cannot equal, at least while the enthusiasm for that cause persists. Thus, in such countries as Russia, Italy, and Germany there may be compensations for the loss of academic freedom. As a matter of fact, we need not confine ourselves to the professor, for social crises and causes release the inhibitions developed in society and give a sense of freedom to people of various circumstances.

Secondly, it is interesting to observe the dependence of the country upon its professors in times of stress. In the comparative routine of peace-time, brains and fact-finders may play no important part, at least no conspicuous part, in the nation's life; but when an emergency impends, trained intelligence is at a premium. The life of society seems to move along sluggishly, even carelessly, the participants uninspired and half asleep. War is declared and we sit upright, startled, and begin to look around for intelligence and efficiency to man the ship of state. Among the war-time crew professors were not wanting.

ACADEMIC FREEDOM IN WAR TIME

When a nation is engaged in warfare, national loyalty swallows up all other ideals. Beside self-preservation, the ideal of freedom pales into insignificance. It has been said that freedom of speech is the first casualty of war. This appears to be a general sociological truth. Conflict groups place loyalty first among their virtues and disloyalty is severely punished. It is the same whether we are

---

* How thin and artificial the academic life appeared to one soldier-professor home from the war is described in a novel by George Boas, *Never Go Back*, Harper's, 1926.

considering a boys' gang or a nation at war.* Apropos of academic freedom during the war, Mr. Angoff writes:

"Bacteriologists, physicists, and chemists vied with philosophers, philologians, and botanists in shouting maledictions upon the Hun, and thousands took to snooping upon such of their brethren as entertained the least doubt about the sanctity of the war. If they could not get overt statements of treason from these heretics, they charged them with the crime of entertaining an 'intellectual attitude' toward the war. Such guilt against American idealism was sufficient cause, in the eyes of all patriotic university presidents and boards of trustees, for the immediate dismissal of the traitor."

He lists fifteen dismissals from our colleges and universities but the list is probably quite incomplete.

By far the largest space in the periodicals was given to the dismissals of Professors Cattell and Dana from Columbia University. In October, 1917, the *Nation* asserted that these dismissals raise an "issue of such far-reaching importance that the real facts of the case should be promptly laid before the public after the most careful study."[10] Were these professors guilty of sedition or merely of bad taste? The whole question at Columbia merges into the general problem of the rights of the minority to be heard in wartime.

"Americans surely do not wish to be as illiberal and intolerant as the Prussians, to whose abominable philosophy and criminal war actions every honest American . . . is absolutely opposed. . . . Shall it be said of the United States, the champion of democracy, that its academic authorities are going to be equally unwise and ungenerous in this war to carry democracy to Germany?"

Three other magazines take a different view of the situation. *World's Work* took the position that "the present proceedings hardly involve this great principle (academic freedom)." Professors Cattell and Dana present a problem of personal conduct, not one of academic freedom. The editor says that Cattell's offense was that he had written letters to Congressmen, on the stationery of Columbia University, asking them to use their in-

* Frederick Thrasher, *The Gang,* Univ. of Chicago, 1927. For an account of the attitudes of various churchmen toward freedom of speech in war-time, see Ray Abrams, *Preachers Present Arms,* Round Table Press, 1933, Chapter VI.

fluence against sending American troops to France. (The *Nation* stated in the article mentioned above that "Professor Cattell declares that he did not urge that our troops should not be sent to France, but only that conscientious objectors to the war should be kept at home.") It is said that Professor Dana was dropped because he "had conspicuously identified himself with the so-called People's Council, an organization whose energies . . . are devoted to obtaining a peace that will be helpful to Germany and damaging to the United States." Has a university any responsibility for the conduct of its professors as men and as citizens?

"Our greatest universities have always insisted that while they give their professors 'academic freedom' in teaching . . . these same professors must maintain a dignity in their personal lives that will not bring the institution into contempt. It is not true that a professor as soon as he leaves the classroom becomes a free agent. . . . The trustees have now dismissed Professors Cattell and Dana because their activities . . . encouraged disloyalty and sedition, and are professedly intended to defeat our military operations and promote the success of Germany. Columbia informs the world that it will harbor no men on its teaching staff and no students who are openly working against the Nation in this, the greatest crisis in its history." [11]

Similar is the attitude of the *Outlook*. It quotes part of the commencement address given by President Butler in June, 1917 to show that the dismissed professors had been amply warned. Dr. Nicholas Murray Butler had said upon that occasion:

" 'So long as national policies were in debate we gave complete freedom, as is our wont, and as becomes a university, but so soon as the Nation spoke by Congress and by the President . . . conditions changed sharply. What had been tolerated before became intolerable now. What had been wrongheadedness was now sedition. What had been folly was now treason. . . . There is, and will be, no place in Columbia University either on the rolls of its Faculties or on the rolls of its students, for any person who opposes or who counsels opposition to the effective enforcement of the laws of the United States or who acts, speaks, or writes treason.' " [12]

The *Outlook* believes that "the right of free speech does not mean irresponsible speech."

"It does not mean that a college professor has a right to take advantage of his position to conduct propaganda against the efficient conduct of the war and use the name of the college in doing so."

The *Independent* differentiates "the legitimate freedom of speech of a citizen in time of war" and "the academic freedom of professors in times of peace." The editor is of the opinion that if the facts are as he understands them, the dismissal of the pacifistic professors from Columbia was "the plain duty of the trustees, and any colleague, student, or citizen who objects to that action and upholds the conduct of the dismissed professors puts himself in the wrong in respect to the paramount duty of loyalty to his Government."

"When a nation is fugitive for its life, or for human liberty, or to save civilization from the destroyer, the supreme duty of every man and woman worthy of the adjective 'human' is to help win the war." [13]

This magazine, however, does not altogether approve of the domination of professorial bodies by trustees, feeling that the faculty is a more adequate body than the business men on the boards of trustees to decide what limitations, regulations, and procedures should govern university teaching. It says that Professor Charles Beard, by his courage and self-sacrifice, has rendered a great public service. Professor Beard resigned from Columbia in the Fall of 1917 as a protest against the high-handedness of the trustees. In December, 1917, he gave out a lengthy statement to the *New Republic* in which he reviewed the history of his grievance in order to indicate that he did not resign in a fit of "unjustified petulance." He cited a number of instances of the subservience of the faculty and of the "humiliating doctrinal inquisition by the trustees." The last of these grievances occurred in the Fall of 1917 and it was more than the eminent historian could endure.

"Early in October, 1917, I was positively and clearly informed . . . that another doctrinal inquisition was definitely scheduled for an early date. It was the evident purpose of a small group of trustees . . . to take advantage of the state of war to drive out or humiliate or terrorize every man who held progressive, liberal, or unconventional views on political matters in no way connected with the war. . . . I therefore tendered my resignation." [14] Professor Beard simply could not abide the expulsion of teachers "without a full and fair hearing by their peers."

The American Association of University Professors met at the University of Chicago in the latter days of December, 1917. At that time a sub-committee of the general committee on academic freedom and academic tenure presented a report on "Academic Freedom in War-time." The *Nation* found their statement quite disappointing, especially the sections dealing with the grounds upon which academic authorities may dismiss faculty members during time of war without prior action by the Government. The editor quotes with approval the statement of Professor Herbert L. Stewart of Dalhousie University who had written in the columns of the same periodical several months before that there is inevitably restraint upon free speech in time of war but that, concerning the exercise of such restraint, "the state is entitled to use it, and no other authority whatsoever." This magazine goes on to relay to its readers the grounds upon which the committee finds that dismissal by academic authorities may be legitimate.*

"(1) Conviction of disobedience to any statute . . . relating to the war; (2) propaganda designed to cause others to resist or evade the compulsory service law . . . (3) action designed to dissuade others from rendering voluntary assistance to the efforts of the Government; (4) University professors of Teutonic extraction . . . violating a parole to avoid . . . hostile acts and utterances concerning the United States." [15]

The editor reiterates that "the essence of university life is freedom to think, freedom to differ." He believes that academic authorities, instead of imposing further restraints, "ought to leave the punishment of law-breakers in the hands of the Government." Thus, he is in open disagreement with the sub-committee of the A.A.U.P. which drew up the report.

Such an expression of opinion does not go unchallenged, particularly during the prosecution of war, and a few weeks later we find a rejoinder by Professor Arthur O. Lovejoy, a member of the committee in question. He admits that the existence of a state of war "entails some exceptional restrictions upon normal freedom of action and utterance" but reminds the readers of the *Nation* that the report insists that these restrictions should not be multiplied, as they tend to be, beyond real necessity. Further, he states that

---

* The entire report was printed in the Bulletin of the A.A.U.P., Vol. 4, 1918, pages 29-47.

the "committee pronounces an emphatic condemnation upon the action of the Columbia trustees" (in dismissing Professor J. M. Cattell). There are, however, the committee holds, "certain acts which in time of war should not be tolerated on the part either of college professors or of other men."

"Such a war as this in which the entire world is involved and the future character of human life and human relations upon this planet is at issue, alters many things and suspends some of the rules of less critical and perilous times. . . . The scholar's freedom, though even now to be protected against all avoidable infringement, must not be converted into a shelter from which, at a time of unprecedented peril and momentousness in the world's history, men may threaten the very existence of the state and weaken the forces upon whose strength and cohesion and eventual triumph the hope of freedom everywhere depends." [16]

Both the *Nation* and the *American Mercury* laud the firm stand of President Lowell of Harvard. The war did not test the Harvard traditions of academic freedom and find them wanting.

"Perhaps the only university president who did not join the traitor-hunt was President Lowell of Harvard. . . . He stood practically alone among his colleagues in his stand for academic freedom, war or no war. But not many were like Lowell. The majority of American learned men hotly repudiated his notion of academic freedom. . . . No wonder Attorney General Palmer found the professors so much to his taste." [17]

There is no necessity to give an extended interpretation of the problem of academic freedom in time of war. It may simply be stated that in such times the restrictive forces normally at work operate with extraordinary intensity.

THE NEW DEAL AND THE BRAIN TRUST

A familiar cartoon to readers of anti-New Deal newspapers is that depicting a forlorn, bespectacled creature clad in academic robes. He is likely to resemble the figure often drawn to represent John Q. Citizen in his expression of frightened confusion and in-effectuality. Indeed, an interesting study of the so-called "brain trust" could be made through an investigation of newspaper comments and cartoons. The results would undoubtedly differ from those obtained in this research, for in the periodicals one does not encounter the venom and invective permeating a number of the newspapers most hostile to the President and his policies. Even those articles and magazines adversely critical are more restrained than many of the newspapers.

It has been popularly assumed that college professors never participated in political affairs before 1933. Such is not the case. Intellectuals in general and professors in particular have long had honorable connections with governmental activities, although, in this country, they have never been so prominent nor excited so much comment as recently. Roger Shaw, in the *Review of Reviews* for June, 1934, tells of "Brain Trusts of History," although he does not distinguish between professors and intellectuals in general. The Washington theorists are not so unusual in their academic approach to public problems, for Europe has had a vast amount of experience with brain trusts in the past. These have often proved "extremely felicitous and successful in their high-minded devotion to public questions of politics, economics, and sociology." In America the original brain trust was "that extraordinary group of practical philosophers who steered the Thirteen Colonies to victory in the American Revolution." The list of these includes Thomas Jefferson, Benjamin Franklin, Alexander Hamilton, the Adams clan, Patrick Henry, James Monroe, James Madison, John Hay, Thomas Paine, John Marshall, George Mason, and a host of others.

"Williamsburg in Virginia was, at that time, the political-minded center of the world; and the theories of John Locke, Jean Jacques Rousseau, Voltaire, Montesquieu, and other 'radicals' of renown were discussed and studied with avidity by the American colonial intelligentsia. . . . That the Tories of 1776 should have feared and hated the Whig brain trust of the American revolution was natural enough. The Whigs were thinking out an epoch-making eighteenth century New Deal."[1]

Brain trusts of other countries are recalled such as the Manchester school in England. Adam Smith, David Ricardo, and John Stuart Mill were successive exponents of Manchester doctrines. Mr. Shaw says that Manchester was progressive in outlook, non-conformist in matters of religion, and opposed to the domination of the English ruling class as an aristocratic oligarchy. These

Manchester economists exerted a powerful influence on the course of English affairs and were, withal, cordially disliked by certain vested interests, especially the Tory agrarian interests. Again, in present-day Russia the "Politburo" constitutes a variety of unofficial brain trust and it "exercises the supreme authority in an advisory capacity." The writer concludes that brain trusts have figured in history consistently and, "in the opinion of many thoughtful minds, a fair share of the uncertain future is theirs."

"Never before has the professorial imprint upon legislative measures been so deep and pervading as now" asserts Albert W. Atwood in the *Saturday Evening Post* in October, 1933 but he reminds us that the scholar has long played an important part in government. He mentions John Quincy Adams, Madison, Monroe, and Jefferson as men "of book-learning as well as political sense."

"Not until Jackson's time did the tradition of dominance by others rather than by scholarly politicians come to prevail. For a long time thereafter, the scholar did not figure much in government." [2]

Yet as the nation grew in economic, social, and political complexity professors came to be identified with all kinds of federal and state commissions. In all the states faculty members have served in various political capacities "without arousing the slightest curiosity." Most of these, as a matter of fact, are wholly known to the public. "But those familiar with the inside operations of government know that these are the strategic men, the ones who do much of the actual work." E. K. Lindley in *Scribner's* agrees that there has been no novelty in the employment of professors in politics. President Hoover used college professors on commissions and appointed them to his cabinet. The advice of our economists has been sought by foreign governments.

"Although a college professorship has not been the usual route to public life in this country, we have had the academic world represented in the elective offices by such men as President Woodrow Wilson, Governors Wilbur Cross and John G. Pollard, and Senators Hiram Bingham and Simeon D. Fess. . . . As Governor of New York, Roosevelt called on Syracuse, Columbia, and Cornell universities . . . yet no one heard of a brain trust." [3]

Practically all of the periodicals concede that the intricacies of modern governmental affairs require the use of numerous trained experts. Franklin Roosevelt has not been unique in valuing the disinterestedness and thoroughness of experts from the universities. Magazine editors and writers have pointed out the desirability of their utilization. The editor of the *Saturday Evening Post* writes,

> "Certainly it is a good practice to use brains in government, in business, in science, in education, in all the activities of life. Nobody objects to, or is criticizing, brains in government. . . . If there are such critics, they must be very stupid persons indeed." [4]

In the same magazine nine months earlier Mr. Atwood had referred to the work of experts from the universities on commissions, in agriculture, taxation, mining, forestry, irrigation, and state institutions of all kinds.

> "The country has no greater asset than its expert, trained, professional government personnel. To conceive of any subject, any piece of legislation . . . regarding which an administration, Republican or Democratic, cannot secure the wisest of advice from experts already in the service, is difficult. It behooves whatever administration is in power to foster, and not to subordinate, this talent . . ."

He does not suggest, however, that only academicians can qualify as experts.

Nobody questions the wisdom and economy of employing experts in private affairs, writes the editor of *Collier's* in May, 1934. Scientists and professors have been indispensable in bringing most of the great industries into existence, and almost every important industry and large corporation today maintains its staff of experts and its research laboratories.

> "The Roosevelt administration has employed its Brain Trust as any modern corporation uses its staff of experts and investigators. How is any administration to know whether a particular suggestion is sound or foolish? The only possible way of getting a reasonable answer is to get the facts." [5]

He considers professors useful because "more than any other class of men they are unprejudiced, or at least not prejudiced by money or business affiliations." Jonathan Mitchell in *Harper's* shows why the government needs the professors.

"What Mr. Roosevelt needed was a neutral someone who did not smell of Wall Street, but who, on the other hand, wouldn't too greatly scare the wealthy."[6]

How did the Roosevelt clique of *academes* come to be? Where did these academic advisers hail from and who are they? Mr. Lindley gives an account of the formation of the little group. It was formed very early in 1932 when Roosevelt began to need data on national problems for his presidential campaign. Samuel Roseman, counsel for Governor Roosevelt, suggested that a competent man be selected to head up this work and, with his chief's assent, he asked Raymond Moley, professor of Public Law at Columbia, to undertake the job. Roseman later explained that Moley was the only one of the few college professors that he knew who seemed to have a level head. Then, Moley scouted among his friends and enlisted Rexford Tugwell, professor of Economics, and Adolf A. Berle, Jr., professor of Law, both of Columbia also. These men canvassed several of their friends but one by one they eliminated most of them "either because they were immersed in doctrines developed in their own specialities or could not simplify and generalize their ideas for the use of Mr. Roosevelt and his campaign." According to Lindley, the phrase "brain trust" was invented by James Kieran of the New York Times. At first its use was resisted but slowly the expression made its way into the public vocabulary. Before long a whole group of professors had descended upon Washington to carry on the work of the new administration. Among this group were M. L. Wilson, Mordecai Ezekiel, W. I. Myers, Herman Oliphant, Gardiner Means, Howard Babcock, O. M. W. Sprague, G. F. Warren, J. H. Rogers, Earle Howard, Leo Wolman, John Dickinson, Isadore Lubin, W. M. W. Splawn, and Arthur Morgan.

The reaction of the country was far from unified. At first Washington seems to have been rather confused by the rapid course of events. In June, 1933, the *Literary Digest* described the "Hullabaloo over the 'Brain Trust.'"

"They're a little dizzy down in Washington trying to keep up with the 'brain trust' . . . Here is a political innovation and nobody knows just what to expect. . . . Is it true that the 'brain trust' is ruling the country behind the White House throne? . . . Everybody, it seems, 'wants to know the professors who are guiding our destinies.' Office-seekers dog their footsteps. Hostesses vie to land them as guests of honor. Professors are the fad."[7]

Mr. Mitchell suggests that perhaps one reason for the bafflement is that the two best-known professorial specimens—George F. Warren and Raymond Moley—are atypical. The latter did not like to be called a professor. At any rate, adds Lindley, "newspaper correspondents examined each Washington arrival to see if he ever taught in a university, had a Ph. D., or by virtue of aptitude for making charts or writing theses could claim academic distinction."[8]

Certain interests in the East may be determined to "get" the professors, writes Louis Fischer in the *Nation,* but the millions seem ready to take a chance on them. "The Brain Trust has a unique opportunity of becoming the trusted servant of America's petty bourgeoisie."[9] Oliver McKee in the *North American Review* agrees that the nation commended the President for drafting scholars. "Here, people said, was convincing evidence that Mr. Roosevelt proposed to run the government far more intelligently than any of his predecessors." During the first year of the Democratic administration, he asserts, the professors rode high on the wave of popular confidence.

"To the man on the street, 'Brain Trust' connoted rain-makers and miracle-workers. The 'college boys', he was sure, had prosperity in their vest pockets."[10]

During the first year of the Democratic regime, wrote George Creel in 1935, "each Brain Truster was a Moses in his own right . . . the nation looked to them for guidance."[11] Similarly, a writer in Alfred Smith's *New Outlook* suggested that the brain trust profited by the mistrust of Wall Street and Congress that followed in the wake of the stock market crash of 1929 and especially by the "revelation of sharp practices on high disclosed before the Senate committee on Banking."

" 'Let's try the professors; they can't be any worse than the bankers,' about sums up the popular attitude during the first few months of the New Deal."[12]

Many liberals no doubt agreed heartily with Oswald Villard's view that the practical men have no right to complain if their powers have fallen into other and idealistic hands.

"We can only be grateful that the United States has turned to college professors, to theoreticians, to closet philosophers. Theirs is a terrific task. But at least we have the consolation that they cannot possibly make a worse mess of it than have the practical men." [13]

It was pointed out in connection with the mobilization of academic talent during the war that there appears to be some tendency for the country to turn to the professors in time of emergency. John Erskine stated in September, 1933, in *Liberty* that "the recent use which President Roosevelt has made of certain professors has done more to redeem the credit of the American college than anything that has happened in a long time." [14] As time went on, several of the periodicals recorded a diminution of confidence in the academic engineers, as we shall see, but in time of stress the country was willing to give the men from the colleges and universities a chance to prove their ability in applying their special knowledge.

On the other hand, the periodicals record the irritation of certain elements in the population. Even before the Democrats took office, there were expressions of hostility. Frederick Prince, a business man, was quoted by *Time* as declaring that "professors are one of the chief curses of the country."

"They talk too much. Most professors are a bunch of cowards and meddlers. . . . You have only to think back over the last ten years to realize the difficulties we have been drawn into through professors. The sooner we get away from their influence, the better." [15]

No doubt this strongly antagonistic attitude was echoed by many other business men in the country. Certainly the swarms of professors in Washington in the early days of the New Deal were, as Mitchell says, alarming and irritating to industrial leaders. Conservatives in Congress and the press, according to Lindley, "railed against the 'theorists' in government . . . that was politer and safer than railing against an extremely popular President."

We have already shown that there was no periodical opposition to the use of experts in political affairs. The crucial question, however, was the extent to which they were dictating or advising policies. The editor of the *Post,* after declaring that we need experts in government, goes on to state that these academic men are more than mere research workers.

"What many people do object to most vigorously is giving vast power and responsibility to academic persons who not only are unaccustomed to either, but who are determined to put over in a time of crisis untested theories, many of which lead toward fundamental changes in our form of government. . . . Professors may be trained to the last point to teach students, or to write books, or even to make investigations for government or for industry. But it does not follow that they are thereby trained to take charge of great agencies for the control of industrial and agricultural affairs . . . " [16]

Forrest Davis, in the *New Outlook* for December, 1933, tells of the "Rise of the Commissars." These new men, Roosevelt's commissars, wield extraordinary power. They formulated the administration's currency and credit policy, the agricultural policy, and, in part at least, the industrial recovery policy.

"Their mathematical formulae outweigh the empirical judgments of politicians and business men. The White House sounds a demand for the unprejudiced 'facts' and a loyal bureaucracy springs to arms with charts. Mark Sullivan, a shrewd traditional journalist, repeatedly insists that the country is being run by statisticians." [17]

Mr. Davis wants to know whether the practical business men and politicians who have ruled the United States are "about to subside before an emergent type of commissar." Are we too, he seems to ask, discarding democracy and an individualistic economy in favor of some form of totalitarian state?

Yet several intimate that the new President was not seeking policy-makers when he gathered together a few men from the campuses. Lindley asserts in *Scribner's:*

"When Roosevelt approved the choice of Moley, he was in search of no theorists; a college professor harboring dogma was the last person he wanted. He wanted a high-grade research assistant and literary secretary."

A moment later, however, he adds that "no list of the six or eight most important architects and builders of the new regime would be valid" without Moley, Tugwell, and Berle. Mitchell in *Harper's* toward the end of 1934 confidently states that "the professors have an immensely important function in the New Deal but theirs is not the dictation of policies." He feels certain that the major policies have been and will be determined by the conflicting pressures brought to bear by the farmers, workers, business, and all the other interest groups. Moreover, adds the editor of the *New Republic,* "insiders in Washington know that the members of this group (the Brain Trust) are far from being in complete accord with one another."[18] *

Although a greater number of the magazines appear sympathetic to the professors in Washington, adverse criticisms are not lacking. In the main, it is said that the academicians in government are impractical, theoretical, and radical. The *New Outlook* describes the condescending attitude of these men toward wealth, the intimation of one professor that the government may be compelled to nationalize certain industries, and their critical attitude toward the profit motive. But the conservatives are already (1933) planning to wage war on the President's brain trusters.

"The brunt of opposition to the Roosevelt program falls on the 'brain trust'. The line of attack of the conservatives is deployed along that sector. The business type, suspicious of formulas, preferring to make instantaneous decisions to meet the problems of the moment, distrusts the intellectual programmist in government . . ."

Oliver McKee in the *North American Review,* October, 1934, believes that, after a year and a half, the popular belief in the infallibility of professorial prescriptions is gone. Not only is the faith in the omniscience of the professors gone but he says that they have become a political liability to the administration.

"The academic life has many virtues, but the environment is not one that enables the average college professor to know at first hand the realities of

---

* Thurman Arnold thinks that the disagreements among New Deal professors only reveal a tendency common to groups of learned men. "Like all groups of learned men since the council of Nicaea, this brain trust split in all directions on doctrinal points. There was a succession of resignations by bright and very articulate men whose pride of opinion had been violated by political action. The brain trust fell into disrepute and became a political liability rather than an asset."

Thurman Arnold, *The Folklore of Capitalism,* Yale Univ. Press, 1937, p. 117.

practical politics. . . . Granted the idealism . . . to administer the affairs of a nation so sectionalized, and with a population so diversified, requires a *Realpolitik* not often found in a college professor." [15]

He claims that many are more apprehensive of what the professors have up their sleeves than of anything that they have done yet. Some of their notions sound very much like Socialist regimentation and planning. The danger is that the academician, in his passion for experiment and his flair for reform, will over-reach himself unless his prescriptions are checked by practical politicians—the Garners, the Snells, the Robinsons, and the Coolidges—and by the business men. This writer also reminds us that there are many professors of equal professional standing to those in Washington who believe that the New Deal policies "will inevitably bring the country to a day of reckoning, if not of grief."

Mr. Atwood, a contributor to the *Saturday Evening Post,* does not wish to make out too good a case against the professor. He admits that there are all types, the old fogies and the young radicals, the cloistered and the practical. Yet he implies a criticism in quoting the remark of another.

"I asked a man who has been both a professor and a government official whether, speaking in the abstract and without any regard to any particular group or administration, he would prefer a government run by professors. His reply was: 'I would not. It would show too little respect for public opinion and prejudices.' The professor is assumed to know everything whereas the better he is, the more he knows about less and less. Very few college positions qualify a man for political work in Washington." [16]

The editor of the same magazine also admits that there are all kinds of professors and of brain trusters; but he devotes more attention in his editorial to those he deems undesirable. These are the ones who have "swelled heads, delusions of grandeur, and self-righteousness." From the rule of such men this country should pray to be delivered.[17] An editorial in *Liberty* urges that we "Get It while the Getting is Good on the Brain Trusters." Bernarr MacFadden tells his readers about the "fantastic theory of recovery originated by the amateur Brain Trusters."

"When men who have no understanding of business principles undertake to manage a business, they are like children lost in the wilderness. They are on their way but they do not know where they are going." [18]

To make matters worse, the professors are cocksure about their fantastic theories and go ahead in a "shambang fashion."

Other editors of mass-circulation magazines are less antagonistic. In 1934, the editor of *Collier's* exhorts his readers to "Trust Brains." He refers to the prejudice against the professor.

"As far back as old men can remember, to call a candidate for public office 'Professor' was to condemn him. When Woodrow Wilson was President, his bitterest enemies referred to him as Professor Wilson. They could put a lot of venom into the word. Of course, nobody would use 'Professor' as a term of contempt if there were no public prejudice to be awakened." [19]

What is the nature of this prejudice? Here again the periodicals suggest an interpretation in terms of the practical tendencies of the Americans. In giving utterance to a few eulogistic remarks upon the "Vanishing Brain Trust," George Creel in *Collier's* for April 13, 1935, admits that these men never sat very well on the stomach of the country. "Farmers and industrialists love to look upon themselves as intensely practical, although they would have a hard time proving it, and entertain a deep-rooted distrust of 'theorists.'" He also believes that Americans are suspicious of book learning.

"We foam over the Little Red School-house and spend money like drunken sailors on junior highs and state universities, but our applause is reserved for those rugged souls who never saw a college." [20]

Two years before, a writer in the *Atlantic Monthly* had pointed to the same factor. Our habit of laughing at the professor as a futile chap betrays a highly significant trait of the American mind— "a tendency to discount the value of thought." This attitude, he explains, is part of the frontier tradition.

"We still reserve our admiration for the doer rather than the thinker. . . . Instinctively we are still more than a little suspicious of learning. Professors are supposed to know more than the common run of men, and since we cannot expect to understand them, we laugh at them and cry them down." [21]

At the conclusion of his brief history of earlier brain trusts in America and elsewhere, Roger Shaw says that these have never been popular with the masses who fail to appreciate "high-brow" aims.

"Demagogic politicians or grasping business interests have usually ranked higher in popular esteem than have thoughtful intellectuals who were striving for the public welfare or for the basic rights of humanity. . . . Brain trusts are frequently prosaic desk-men whose appeal to the popular imagination is absent. Their academic attitude toward vital problems annoys opponents." [22]

If, as one writer suggests, war on the brain trust is one of the expressions of the conflict between the old political regime and the new, we may expect the periodicals interested in furthering the new regime to lend support to the professors. In June, 1933, the *New Republic* carried an editorial on the subject in which it defended the belabored ones from the criticisms of the daily press. It is said that "more improvement has taken place since the expert advisers went to work than in any other similar period of the entire depression." As to the comparative fitness of the professor in relation to the practical men, we are told that "practical men were in control of the government for many years prior to March 4, 1933, and how close they came to wrecking our society completely is known to all newspaper readers." [23] More vehement is the statement a few months later of Bruce Bliven. He denies that professors are "fuzzy-minded incompetents"; in fact, he sees no reason why this country could not be run by them as well as or better than by the "masterful lords of industry."

"In my life I have met a great many professors; and through the accident of journalistic work it also happens that I have met and talked at length with perhaps eighteen of the twenty leading industrialists of the country. These great industrialists show no higher average of executive competence, in my opinion, than do an equal number of outstanding professors. What the industrialists have is stubborn egoism and lack of imagination." [24]

"Look over the world wherever you may, and the practical men are utterly at a loss," comments Mr. Villard in the *Nation*. Since both the war and the depression tested them and found them wanting, they have no right to complain if their powers have fallen into idealistic hands.

In the same vein of sympathetic interpretation, a "Washington Observer" in the *Review of Reviews* defends the academic politicians from the charge of impracticality. To be sure, they believe that the age of rugged individualism must be supplanted by one

in which the government becomes an "active and sympathetic participant in the serious business of living and letting live."

"They may be dreamers but even their dreams are realistic. They are slightly cynical, hard-boiled, and practical. If they have any illusions they are of a kind shared by the majority which placed Franklin D. Roosevelt in the White House." [25]

Similarly, the *Literary Digest* grants that they may be impractical; they may be too theoretical and devoted to "certain disquieting 'isms.'"

"But they are an intelligent, an unselfish, an honest, and a loyal lot. And it is no wonder that Mr. Roosevelt finds more satisfaction in turning to them for counsel than to the hack politicians that have infested Washington for generations." [26]

Finally, a writer in *Harper's* exhorts us not to shoot the professors and tells why the government needs them.

"If the Federal government henceforth is to fix limits to the destructiveness of private competition and impose a peace of governmental regulation upon us, more and more college professors must go to Washington until, in the future, we shall succeed in building for ourselves a professorial American civil service, supported by its own loyalties and traditions." [27]

Mr. Creel claims that the second stage of the New Deal has been reached (1935) and that the need now is for those with ability of the administrative type who can put the plans into operation. "The Brain Trust passed because its job was done." Trails have been blazed and now the solid building begins. With penetrating insight, he concludes,

"The real criticism of the 'brain trust' comes from those who feel that the whole course of the administration is hostile to their special and private interests. It is not the fact that some of the presidential advisers are college professors that constitutes the real grievance of the critics. It is that with his collegiate advisers the President is taking some steps which he might easily have taken without them—toward remedying a few of the most glaring inequalities in the distribution of the income in this country."

Here again we are faced with the facts, well-known to the sociologist, that people think in terms of interests rather than of abstract principles. Many cannot decide what attitude to take toward the professor in politics until informed on the nature of the policies contemplated by him and his academic brethren. Once informed, each one entertaining definite political convictions of any complexion must only cast around for a suitably high-sounding phraseology with which to clothe his rationalizations.

REFERENCES

The War

[1] *New Republic,* X, 308, 1917.
"Who Willed American Participation?"

[2] *American Mercury,* XI, 414, 1927.
"The Historians Cut Loose," C. Hartley Grattan.

[3] *American Mercury,* XI, 177, 1927.
"The Higher Learning Goes to War," Charles Angoff.

[4] *Atlantic Monthly,* CXXIII, 537, 1919.
"The Demobilized Professor."

[5] *Review of Reviews,* LVIII, 68, 1918.
"War Work of the University of Wisconsin," Charles R. Van Hise.

[6] *Scribner's,* LXIII, 77, 1918.
"The American College and the Great War," Robert L. Kelley.

[7] *Scribner's,* LXV, 465, 1919.
"The Professor and the Wide, Wide World," Gordon H. Gerould.

[8] *Harper's,* CXLVI, 14, 1922.
"What is Education," Arthur T. Hadley.

[9] See No. 4.

[10] *Nation,* CV, 388, 1917.
"The Case of the Columbia Professors."

[11] *World's Work,* XXXV, 123, 1917.
"The Columbia Professors and Academic Freedom."

[12] *Outlook,* CXVII, 238, 1917.
"Free Speech."

[13] *Independent,* XCII, 118, 1917.
"The Public, the University, and the Professor."

[14] *New Republic,* XIII, 249, 1917.
"A Statement," Charles A. Beard.

[15] *Nation,* CVI, 255, 1918.
"The Professors in Battle Array."

[16] *Nation,* CVI, 401, 1918.
"Letter to the Editor," Arthur O. Lovejoy.

[17] See No. 3.

Brain Trust

[1] *Review of Reviews,* LXXXIX, 25, 1934.
"Brain Trusts of History," Roger Shaw.

[2] *Saturday Evening Post,* CCVI, October 14, 1933.
"Government by Professors," Albert W. Atwood.

[3] *Scribner's,* XCIV, 257, 1933.
"War on the Brain Trust," E. K. Lindley.

[4] *Saturday Evening Post,* CCVII, July 28, 1934.
"Brains in Government."

[5] *Collier's,* May 19, 1934.
"Trust Brains."

[6] *Harper's,* CLXVIII, 740, 1934.
"Don't Shoot the Professors," Jonathan Mitchell.

[7] *Literary Digest,* CXVI, June 3, 1933.
"The Hullabaloo over the Brain Trust."

[8] See No. 3.

[9] *Nation,* CXXXVI, 604, 1933.
"Social Change in the Brain Trust," Louis Fischer.

[10] *North American Review,* CCXXXVIII, 340, 1934.
"Professors Put to the Test," Oliver McKee.

[11] *Collier's,* April 13, 1935.
"Vanishing Brain Trust," George Creel.

[12] *New Outlook,* CLXII, 23, 1933.
"The Rise of the Commissars," Forrest Davis.

[13] *Nation,* CXXXVII, October 4, 1933.
"The Idealist comes to the Front," O. G. Villard.

[14] *Liberty,* September 16, 1933.
"What Price Education?" John Erskine.

[15] *Time,* XXI, 42, 1933.
"Professors vs. Frederick Prince."

[16] See No. 4.

[17] See No. 12.

[18] *New Republic,* LXXV, 85, 1933.
"The Brain Trust."

[19] See No. 10.

[20] See No. 2.

[21] See No. 4.

[22] *Liberty,* March 21, 1936.
"Get it while the Getting is Good on the Brain Trusters," Bernarr MacFadden.

[23] See No. 5.

[24] See No. 11.

[25] *Atlantic Monthly,* CLII, 124, 1933.
"The Professor's Dilemma."

[26] See No. 1.

[27] See No. 14.

[28] *New Republic,* LXXVI, 11, 1933.
"Washington Kaleidoscope," Bruce Bliven.

[29] *Review of Reviews,* LXXXVII, 20, 1933.
"A Brain Trust that Works."

[30] *Literary Digest,* CXVI, 10, 1933.
"The Brain Trust."

[31] See No. 6.

CHAPTER VI

Analysis and Interpretation

I. Distribution of Material

Table II indicates the distribution of data by magazine and subject. In the exploratory phases of the investigation perhaps one hundred additional articles were read and abstracted but had to be discarded before final outlines were made because of their irrelevance. It will be noted that the mass-circulation magazines, the *American, Collier's, Liberty, Literary Digest,* and *Saturday Evening Post,* contain relatively few articles, while, at the other extreme, the *Nation* carries almost twenty-five percent of the total. This distribution gives a bias to the study that is particularly noticeable in regard to the discussion of academic freedom. (A discussion of this bias is presented in the last section of this chapter.) Table III shows the circulations of the respective magazines and these figures may be related to the distribution of data.

TABLE II

Magazine	Personality	Salary and Life	Academic Freedom	Teaching and Research	Political Affairs	Totals
American	.	5	.	1	.	6
American Mercury	2	2	2	.	.	6
Atlantic Monthly	9	5	6	11	2	33
Century	2	3	3	4	.	12
Collier's	1	3	.	.	3	7
Forum	5	5	2	4	.	16
Harper's	8	5	8	2	2	25
Independent	.	6	15	2	.	23
Liberty	.	.	1	1	2	4
Literary Digest	.	10	15	2	4	31
Nation	6	26	47	4	8	91
New Republic	2	5	22	3	7	39
North American Review	1	3	.	2	1	7
Outlook	1	4	5	3	1	14
Review of Reviews	1	2	.	2	3	8
Saturday Evening Post	1	2	2	1	5	11

Scribner's	6	5	4	2	2	19
Time	.	3	1	2	.	6
World's Work	3	8	2	4	.	17
Totals	48	102	135	50	40	375

TABLE III

Magazine Circulations in Thousands

	1914	1930
American	320	2,230
American Mercury	..	67
Atlantic Monthly	28	133
Century	70	20
Collier's	562	1,967
Forum	..	91
Harper's	100	121
Independent	28	..
Liberty	..	1,941
Literary Digest	259	1,401
Nation	38*	38
New Republic	37*	12
North American Review	15	..
Outlook	125	85
Review of Reviews	175	178
Saturday Evening Post	1,986	2,908
Scribner's	150	91
Time	..	225
World's Work	105	146

(N. W. Ayer and Son, *Directory of Newspapers and Periodicals*).

* Figures for 1920.

Nor do we find uniformity in the distribution of material through time. Table IV shows the spread of the articles in five-year intervals.

TABLE IV

CHRONOLOGICAL DISTRIBUTION OF MATERIAL, 1890-1938

1890-94.	5
1895-99.	12
1900-04.	20
1905-09.	29
1910-14.	42
1915-19.	69
1920-24.	57
1925-29.	55
1930-34.	53
1935-38.	33
Total	375

The number of articles obtained during the decade before 1900 probably would have been greater if several of the magazines studied had had more complete indexes. Indeed, in a few cases periodicals could not be obtained in Philadelphia for the period before 1900.* The steady increase of material in every successive period until 1920 is partly explicable by the appearance of new magazines on the market. The war and the high cost of living go far to account for the fact that the period, 1915-19, shows the largest number of articles.

Table V presents an analysis according to the occupation of the writers.

TABLE V

OCCUPATION OF PERIODICAL WRITERS, 1890-1938

	Professors	Journalists	Presidents and Deans	Misc.
Personality	26	9	. .	13
Salary and Life	43	39	11	19
Academic Freedom . . .	38	73	11	13

* In the collection of data the facilities of three libraries were utilized: Free Library of Philadelphia, University of Pennsylvania Library, and Temple University Library.

Teaching	26	7	9	13
Politics	3	27	2	3
Totals	136	155	33	61
% distribution	35.3	40.3	8.6	15.8

It will be noted that more than one-third of the articles were written by professors. A somewhat greater number were written by members of editorial staffs and others listed as journalists by *Who's Who in America*. The miscellaneous column includes occasional business and professional men and women, professional writers of various kinds, and those whose occupation is unknown. Anonlymous writers posing as professors were so recorded, although one may object to this procedure.

II. ANALYSIS AND INTERPRETATION OF PERIODICAL ATTITUDES

It will be necessary to deal separately with the attitudes expressed toward the various aspects of the academic profession. In general, however, there are two factors that must be taken into account in any interpretation of the material. The first is cultural, the other socio-psychological. The cultural factor is somewhat vague but very important. An analysis of societal values, such as Sumner's *Folkways,* seems fairly clear when we look at the comparatively homogeneous cultures of primitive people but it presents many difficulties when applied to our own society, marked as it is by heterogeneity and rapid change. In America there are class differences, differences based upon race and nationality, religion, education, and geography. Generalization becomes difficult and unwarranted, under such conditions. Nevertheless, one can hardly deny that our frontier traditions and commercialism are important in explaining the attitude toward the orthodox learning of the schools. In order to understand the high regard for the "practical" and the disparagement of the "theoretical," one must know the history of America. Attitudes develop in a specific social context. This is equally true of a society or an individual. On the other hand, our American culture seems to show ambivalence of attitude toward the schools, for, while we minimize matters and persons academic, school enrollments are very large and have increased greatly in recent decades. This apparent ambivalence has been pointed out by several sociologists. Sumner has said that, while we laud education and multiply educational institutions, we also reserve much of our admiration for the "common man" who is said to be wiser than the learned philosophers.* The Lynds suggest that "this thing, education, appears to be desired frequently not for its specific content but as a symbol—by the working class as an open sesame that will mysteriously admit their children to a world closed to them, and by the business class as a heavily sanctioned aid in getting on further economically or socially in the world."†

Concerning the socio-psychological factor, it should be said that the tendency in popular discussion is to stress problems or difficulties. Magazine accounts seldom attempt to present thorough-going and systematic analyses of the subject in hand because of the necessity for brevity and the desire to retain the interest of their readers. Moreover, it is easier to write about the problem aspect of a subject for the reason that we are more likely to be aware of this aspect. This is particularly true in the case of professors writing about their own profession. Those with personal problems in relation to the environment may quickly accumulate data that may form the basis for an article. E. T. Krueger, referring to the tension in the maladjusted person, says that "the writing of life-history documents by persons under mental tension is also a phenomenon of confession. . . . Life-history documents, therefore, comprise one form of behavior by which relief is secured from mental tension."* Thus, more or less maladjusted professors may

---

* W. G. Sumner, *Folkway's*, Ginn, 1906, pp. 205-206.

† *Middletown*, op. cit., p. 219.

* E. T. Krueger, *Autobiographical Documents and Personality*, unpublished Ph. D. thesis, Univ. of Chicago, 1925, page 57.

A limitation of "insight" analyses of socio-psychological data may be noted here. Perplexed and maladjusted persons may be motivated to study those situations and institutions which constitute the environmental source of the problem or problems. The reason for this tendency is that their social difficulties have induced a great deal of thinking along a particular line, according to a pattern outlined by Dewey in *"How We Think."* Such persons, however, may bring a distinct bias to bear on their interpretations in the form of rationalizations; or, at least, the data are so selected that only one aspect is presented, though there are pretensions of completeness.

write of those phases of the profession that touch them intimately and unpleasantly. This becomes more plausible when we consider the literary propensities of many academicians and their willingness, unlike the members of other, more commercialized professions, to present their discussions to the public. In general the author believes that this socio-psychological factor has given a certain bias to the whole account.

A Note on the Method of Analysis

The data of this study have been classified into three categories. A larger number of categories might have been utilized but such an elaboration did not seem necessary and would have only made the work highly complicated. The majority of articles are of the "for" or "against" type. As the tables indicate, a few articles are classified as "neutral" either because they are without attitudinal slant or because the remarks "for" and "against" seem to balance. No attempt was made to evolve a complicated technique in which paragraphs, sentences, or descriptive terms are classified into a number of categories. The author simply classified the abstracts of articles as impartially as possible, noting the descriptive terms employed as well as the general context. A more detailed technique, of course, could not have avoided the factor of judgment in assigning data to a particular category nor could it have ignored the general context which helps to determine the meanings of words, sentences, and paragraphs. As a matter of fact, the majority of popular articles are organized around a particular attitude so that the problem of classification was not especially difficult. It would have been desirable to have other competent workers classify the data as a check upon the author but this was not feasible in view of the great amount of labor involved.*

---

* For a more elaborate technique of handling periodical data, see Hornell Hart, *"Changing Opinions About Business Prosperity: A Consensus of Magazine Opinion in the U. S. 1929-32"* Am. Jour. of Sociology, XXXVIII, 665.

Also, by the same writer, *Recent Social Trends,* McGraw Hill Book Co., 1933, Chapter 8.

A. THE ACADEMIC PERSONALITY

TABLE VI

ATTITUDES TOWARD THE ACADEMIC PERSONALITY

	Academic Writers	Non-Academic Writers	Total
Favorable	6	7	13
Neutral	3	3	6
Unfavorable	18	11	29
Totals	27	21	48

	Authors	Non-Academic writers Journalists	Business	Misc.
Favorable	1	4	1	1
Neutral	.	2	.	1
Unfavorable	2	3	3	3
Totals	3	9	4	5

Table VI constitutes an attitudinal analysis of the material on
personality. It will be noted that over one-half of the articles were
written by professors and that these show a higher percentage of
unfavorable attitudes (67%) than those written by non-academic
writers (52%). In spite of the American interest in education,
are we not likely to disparage intellectuality and intellectual persons? We are a so-called practical people who admire action
rather than thought. Is not this cultural attitude reflected in the
periodical evaluations of the professorial personality? Also, we
refer again to the socio-psychological factor mentioned above.
Those who are maladjusted are likely to be motivated to write out
their grievances against their colleagues (and themselves) whereas
better-adjusted professors have fewer mental conflicts and thus
are not so likely to take pen in hand. With reference to the whole
group of articles it may be suggested, in addition, that there are
other reasons why the adversely critical articles are more numerous.
There are occupational prejudices that cannot be overlooked;
editors are not academic people, nor are most of the readers of
the general magazines. Again, it seems true that a popular article

is more attractive when written along a particular bias. Scientific statements are likely to be heavy with qualifications, impersonal, sober, and thus unattractive to the general reader. The bias of adverse criticism seems to furnish special opportunities for clever quips and witticisms, for these flourish in a soil of disparagement. In addition, strongly critical articles are startling and tend to gain the reader's attention more quickly.

Can we draw any conclusions concerning professorial prestige from these results? Reflection on this point leads to the inference that there is no necessary correlation between criticism of the psychological characteristics of an occupational type and occupational status. Various types of political, commercial, and professional leaders may be criticized unfavorably as persons but their status is unquestionably high. Indeed, there appears to be some tendency to criticize most vigorously those in eminent positions, the lesser men not being of sufficient importance to merit unfavorable comment. Probably no one has taken the trouble to write about the psychological characteristics of truck-drivers. One study of occupational prestige placed the professor second among the professions, although the study did not include a sufficient number of the more important business and governmental positions.* Thus our inference is corroborated.

It is interesting to note, further, that of twelve articles referring to changes in academic types, all but three specifically state that the trend is toward a more practical type. This statement occurs as early as 1902 and as late as 1935.

The median year for the articles of favorable attitude is 1919 and for those of unfavorable attitude 1922. It is difficult to know what significance, if any, attaches to this fact.

B. SALARY

As indicated in Chapter 2, the periodicals believe overwhelmingly that academic salaries are inadequate. Table VII reveals how one-sided the results are. (Nevertheless, it is worth noting that six professors consider salaries adequate.)

---

* Georg W. Hartman, *"The Prestige of Occupation,"* Personnel Journal, XIII, Oct., 1934.

TABLE VII

ATTITUDES TOWARD ACADEMIC SALARIES

	Professors	Journalists	College Presidents	Misc.	Totals
Adequate	6	.	1	1	8
Neutral	1	2	.	.	3
Inadequate	19	28	8	7	62
Totals	26	30	9	8	73

In interpreting this emphasis upon the economic deficiencies of the academic profession, one must recall what was said above concerning the tendency of the magazines to deal with the "problem" aspects of social phenomena. This factor gives a bias to the account at the very outset. Again, in regard to professors writing about academic salaries, those with grievances are likely to predominate. Professors who consider themselves well-paid are not likely to take pen in hand for purposes of composing a magazine article whereas the other group, feeling abused, are irritated to the point of such composition. This principle was emphasized by an older school of functional psychologists. Tension (maladjustment, irritation, frustration, etc.) provokes the individual to thought. Another element in the interpretation of professorial dissatisfaction with salaries concerns his standard of living. Miss Peixotto states that "the professor's ways of living tend now toward the standards and ways of the world at large. . . . In the world, 'academics', hitherto relatively isolated, meet the so-called 'upward' trend in the standard of living that has touched all of us."* With the widespread distribution of the material things of life made possible by large-scale production has probably come a keener realization, on the part of the professor, of his economic limitations. Higher standards of living in America have tended undoubtedly to increase his dissatisfaction. Everyone wants an automobile, a radio, an oil-burner, European travel, etc.—and so does the professor. If he is more practical-minded than formerly, we cannot expect him to retain the simple tastes of the ascetic.

* Op. cit. page 10.

The expression of these attitudes is not haphazard but is related to the business cycle. This can be shown by selecting a group of magazines published throughout the entire period 1900-1934,* counting the number of articles in these which consider salary inadequate, and comparing with cost of living indexes. Table VIII indicates that, with the sole exception of the period, 1905-09, the curves of distribution rise and fall together.

TABLE VIII

"INADEQUATE" SENTIMENT AND THE COST OF LIVING

	No. of articles	Cost of living†
1900-04	3	80
1905-09	10	87
1910-14	5	96
1915-19	6	134
1920-24	9	177
1925-29	7	171
1930-34	4	140

C. LIFE

The paucity of material dealing with academic life makes detailed analysis impractical. Table IX shows an analysis of the attitudes expressed and the occupation of the writers.

TABLE IX

ATTITUDES TOWARD ACADEMIC LIFE

	Prof.	Journalists	Business	Misc.	Total
Favorable	9	2	.	.	11
Neutral	1	1	.	1	3
Unfavorable	2	2	3	1	8
Totals	12	5	3	2	22

* The following magazines have been published continuously from 1900 to 1934: *American, Atlantic Monthly, Forum, Harper's, Literary Digest, Outlook, Nation, Review of Reviews, Saturday Evening Post,* and *Scribner's.*

† Cost of living averages for these periods have been computed from Paul Douglas' *Real Wages in the U. S.,* Houghton Mifflin Co., 1930, p. 60, and the more recent figures of the National Industrial Conference Board.

D. ACADEMIC FREEDOM

Reference to Table II will show that slightly over one-half of the articles dealing with academic freedom emanate from the *Nation* and *New Republic,* two militantly "liberal" magazines. This, of course, gives a distinct bias to the results. Yet the author knows of no satisfactory method of coping with this problem. To eliminate these two altogether does not seem warranted. Weighting the data according to magazine circulation is pseudo-scientific, for as we shall see in the last section, little or nothing is known concerning the relations of reader opinion and magazine opinion. Moreover, even assuming there were a significant correlation between the opinion of magazine and readers, it is still true that in the formation of public opinion not all persons are equally influential. A small group of teachers and writers may wield an influence far out of proportion to their numbers.

Table X gives the distribution through time of data dealing with academic freedom in the same selected group of magazines as was used in Table VIII.

TABLE X

CHRONOLOGICAL DISTRIBUTION OF ATTITUDES

TOWARD ACADEMIC FREEDOM

	Unfavorable	Favorable	Neutral	Total
1900-04	2	3	1	6
1905-09	1	3	.	4
1910-14	1	7	.	8
1915-19	2	19	4	25
1920-24	.	10	2	12
1925-29	1	7	1	9
1930-34	1	7	3	11
Total	8	56	11	75

It is not surprising that we find the war period, 1915-1919, to be the modal point of the distribution. Moreover, if the war period is eliminated from consideration because of its uniqueness, it is to be noted that during the first fifteen years of the century, 1900-1914 inclusive, 13 articles were favorable to academic freedom, whereas in the fifteen years, 1920-1934, there were 24. Indeed, during the three years, 1935-1937 inclusive, there were 10 articles. What do these results signify? It is not easy to answer this question but, at least, we may suggest possible factors and hypotheses. One possible variable is editorial policy, although no knowledge of this factor could be obtained. Quite possibly the results point to a greater awareness of the importance of the issue on the part of certain segments of our population. Since 1920 the world has witnessed a steady march toward regimentation of thought and, perhaps consequently, a more strenuous effort on the part of the magazines in this country, at least those included in this study, to defend democratic principles. Also, the magazines are sensitive to public interest and perhaps the increased attention to the subject of academic freedom is symptomatic of greater interest in, and a realization of the importance of, academic freedom on the part of the American public. Possibly too the results point to growing restriction upon freedom in American colleges and universities. The large number of articles since 1935 were, for the most part, protests against oath laws for teachers. It should be added that the results might have been different if data on dismissals had been included.

TABLE XI

ATTITUDES TOWARD ACADEMIC FREEDOM, 1890-1938*

	Prof.	Journalists	College Presidents	Misc.	Totals
Favorable	35	50	7	6	98
Unfavorable	2	5	3	5	15
Neutral	1	18	1	2	22
Totals	38	73	11	13	135

* An article was classified as favorable to academic freedom if it expressed the opinion that the teacher or research worker should be free from any interference in regard to his teaching, investigations, or publications. Articles urging some type of modification to this principle (other than judgment of competence by qualified members of the academic profession) were considered unfavorable.

Obviously, the favorable attitude predominates, particularly among the professors. It should be emphasized, however, that these are paper attitudes only. Those who write in favor of full academic freedom and those who read with approval what is written may behave in ways quite inconsistent with their theoretical attitude of approval. We are dealing here with speech reactions only. It is well known how actual cases of dismissal or intimidation reveal many spurious brands of democratic liberalism among the faculty.

E. Teaching and Research

Table XII analyzes the attitudes expressed on the teaching-research issue. The majority favor emphasis upon teaching rather than research and specialized scholarship. This does not necessarily mean that these writers would accord no place to research but rather that they consider the emphasis in recent decades upon research and specialized scholarship to be unjustified. The academic writers themselves favor teaching or are protesting against academic scholarship. The general magazines provide refuge for such grievances.

TABLE XII

Attitudes Toward Teaching and Research, 1890-1938

	Prof.	College Presidents and Deans	Journalists	Misc.	Totals
Teaching	15	4	3	4	26
Research	6	3	1	1	11
Middle Ground	4	4	2	3	13
Totals	25	11	6	8	50

The chronological distribution of these attitudes shows no significant modal points.

F. Political Affairs

The paucity of data relative to the World War does not justify statistical analysis; therefore in this section we shall analyze only the attitudes toward the Brain Trust.

Table XIII indicates clearly that the periodicals were not hostile, in the main, to the academic experts participating in New Deal politics. Sixty percent were favorable and twenty-four percent unfavorable. In the mass-circulation magazines *(Collier's, Liberty, Literary Digest* and *Saturday Evening Post)* four articles were unfavorable and five favorable. In the remainder, which may be called the intellectual magazines, only two articles were opposed to the Brain Trust, while ten were favorable. It is interesting to note further that only one of the twenty-five articles was written by a college professor. Twenty-two were written by journalists.

TABLE XIII

ATTITUDES TOWARD THE BRAIN TRUST

Favorable	15
Unfavorable	6
Neutral	4
	25

III. THE SOCIOLOGICAL SIGNIFICANCE OF MAGAZINE ATTITUDES

The problem of the significance of the foregoing results as an index of social attitudes is a complex one. The author has made a large number of inquiries and has carried on an extensive search for "leads" but the findings are disappointing.* First of all, is there a significant correlation between the attitudes expressed in the various periodicals and the attitudes of the respective readers of these same periodicals? If so, we could at least discover the attitudes of that large segment of the population which may be called the magazine public. (The attitudes of each magazine would have to be weighted in accordance with its circulation.) However, no specific information could be obtained on this point. It is true

---

* The author has consulted a number of sources in the attempt to secure information which would aid in the interpretation of his analyses. Among these are such commercial research agencies as R. L. Polk, Daniel Starch, and the commercial research department of the Curtis Publishing Co. All such studies, however, are primarily for advertisers and analyses are given in terms of buying power rather than of social attitudes.

that editors secure reactions from their readers in the form of letters but how significant are, let us say, fifty letters among fifty thousand readers? Moreover, there is probably a greater tendency for those who are opposed to a particular article to write such letters. One can draw no positive conclusions here. If, for example, one article evokes twenty-five letters of protest and another two hundred, we have no basis for concluding that the latter does greater violence to the attitudes of the whole group of readers. A flood of letters may signify that a vested interest has been attacked, which, although small in numbers, may be especially sensitive to criticism. The editor, from a practical point of view, may take heed but he has no real knowledge of the reactions of the great majority of his readers. One journalist has said that "every magazine is endeavoring to meet the needs of a more or less restricted group of readers, whose tastes determine its policy."* But the question remains as to what extent the editorial effort to please reader tastes results in conformity of the articles published to the attitudes of these readers. Reader "taste" and editorial "policy" assuredly encompass much more than the matter of attitudes. This is not to suggest that social attitudes are never important in editorial policy but only that we have here no valid basis for generalization.† As a matter of fact, it would be impossible for an editor to publish only those articles that appealed to all of his readers. His aim, rather, is to offer a variety of attractions, hoping that something will whet the interest of each group among the subscribers.

"In every issue, each special group of readers will find something that they will not care for. But if the editor has been skillful, there will be something to interest every group of readers; and there will be nothing that fails to appeal to some group."‡

However, we cannot assume that the selection of material for a general periodical is a matter to be settled by the editor alone, who

---

* John Bakeless, *Magazine Making,* Viking Press, 1931, page 164.

† Cf. G. A. Lundberg, *"The Newspaper and Public Opinion,"* Social Forces, IV, 709, 1926. Lundberg found wide discrepancies between reader and newspaper opinions.

‡ Bakeless, op. cit., pp. 172-73.

is thinking only of his readers. There are advertisers to be considered. Indeed, Bakeless claims that the advertiser rules supreme. "Since the average periodical exists solely by virtue of the advertising contracts which he, or his agent, places, the whole management is necessarily directed to satisfying his demands."* Hornell Hart suggests the same influence and adds several others.

"The content of most magazines is determined by a careful calculation of reader reaction, but other forces also are at work in determining what shall be printed. It has frequently been charged that the contents of newspapers and magazines are determined to a greater or lesser degree by the machinations of public relations counsels and pressure groups. Furthermore, there are such matters as the influence of advertisers and the whole complex of social and editorial taboos . . ."†

About all that can be said on this point is that the general magazines present discussions of issues and problems of current *interest* to a large number of readers, although interest implies no agreement in attitude. One may be interested in a discussion while disagreeing with the attitude of the discussant; in fact, one way to arouse interest is that of presenting interpretations that diverge to a degree from those commonly held.

If we can give no confident answer to the problem of the correlation between magazine attitudes and reader attitudes, how much can be said on the relation of magazine attitudes to public opinion in general? The *Recent Social Trends* report on changing attitudes and interests suggests that the sociologist may regard the volumes of the leading periodicals in much the same way as the geologist looks at the strata of the earth's crust. "Here are precipitated layers of evidence about the intellectual and emotional life of past years."‡ Yet we have already stated that a differentiation must be made between "interest" and "attitude". "Evidence about the intellectual and emotional life of past years" may refer to either. Of course, this report has a much broader scope than the present study so that conclusions for one are not necessarily valid for the other.

---

* *Magazine Making,* op. cit., page 11.
† *Recent Social Trends,* McGraw Hill, 1933, page 386.
‡ Ibid., page 382.

At one point in Hart's report on "Changing Social Attitudes and Interests" he was able to say that the conclusions from magazine material agreed with a *Literary Digest* poll on the subject of prohibition but, in general, he remains dubious as to the sociological significance of his findings.

"In view of the immense complexity of the problem of attitude measurement, it has been deemed wise merely to present significant data about the relative amounts of attention devoted to certain selected topics, accompanied by an attempt to analyze the frequency with which favorable and unfavorable opinion indicators occur. *It must be emphasized that the social significance of the trends and fluctuations revealed is a matter which is left for the reader to determine.*† (Italics mine.)

A third problem in regard to the sociological significance of periodical material relates to the effect upon attitudes. For their readers the magazines constitute one type of environmental influence, although exact measurement is difficult or impossible at present. Thus, it may be said that the general magazines have been a factor in molding public opinion in regard to the academic profession. The articles analyzed in this study, it may be assumed, have helped to create popular stereotypes of the college professor and his work. To be sure, the readers of the magazines included in the present analysis are a limited group but, being largely readers of the more intellectual publications in the field, they represent a selected group whose influence is likely to be greater than their numerical important would indicate.

Before periodicals can be utilized more effectively in sociological research, direct investigation must be made of the processes of magazine making, reading habits of magazine readers, and the social attitudes of various groups in society. All such studies would give a more scientific basis for the interpretation of the periodical material that has been analyzed in the foregoing pages.

---

† Ibid., page 387.

SELECTED BIBLIOGRAPHY

GENERAL REFERENCES

Bibliographies of Research Studies in Education. (U. S. Office of Education.)
Bulletins of the American Association of University Professors.
Bulletins of the Association of American Colleges.
The Journal of Higher Education.
References on Higher Education, Library Leaflet, No. 35. (Bureau of Education, September, 1927.)

HISTORY OF HIGHER EDUCATION

Bibliography, Review of Educational Research, October, 1936.
Canby, Henry, *Alma Mater,* Farrar and Rinehart, 1936.
Duggan, Stephen P., "History and Present Tendencies of the American College," in Klapper, Paul (ed.) *College Teaching,* World Book Co., 1920.
McGrath, Earl, *Evolution of Administrative Officers in Institutions of Higher Education in the U. S. 1860-1933,* Unpub. Doctor's Thesis, Univ. of Chicago, 1936.
Sharpless, Isaac, *The American College,* Doubleday Page, 1915, pp. 3-43.
Thwing, C. F., *History of Higher Education in America,* Appleton, 1906.
Wills, Elbert, *Growth of American Higher Education,* Dorrance, 1936.

ACADEMIC PERSONALITY

Waller, W. W., *Sociology of Teaching,* Wiley, 1932, Part V, "What Teaching does to Teachers."

SALARY AND LIFE

American Association of University Professors (Committee Y), *Depression, Recovery and Higher Education,* McGraw Hill, 1937.
Arnett, Trevor, *Teachers' Salaries,* General Education Board, 1928.
Barrows, David, "What are the Prospects of a University Professor?" Univ. of California Chronicle, April, 1922.
Boothe, Viva, *Salaries and the Cost of Living in Twenty-seven State Universities and Colleges 1913-1932,* Ohio State Univ. Press, 1932.
Clark, Harold, *Life Earnings in Selected Occupations in the U. S.,* Harper and Brothers, 1937.
Davis, C. O., "Teaching Load in a University," *School and Society,* XIX, 311, 1924.
Douglas, Paul, *Real Wages in the U. S. 1890-1926,* Houghton Mifflin, 1930.
Faris, E., "Too Many Ph. D's?" *American Journal of Sociology,* XXXIX, 509, 1934.
Gray, William S., (ed.) *Needed Readjustments in Higher Education,* Univ. of Chicago Press, 1933, Chapter 2.
Greenleaf, Walter J., *College Salaries, 1936,* U. S. Office of Education, Bull. 1937, No. 9.
Haggerty, Melvin, *The Evaluation of Higher Institutions,* (Vol. 2, The Faculty), Univ. of Chicago, 1937, Chapter 6.
Harris, R. G., "The Doctorate and the Depression," *School and Society,* XXXVI, 498.
Henderson, Y., "Quality vs. Quantity in University Faculties," Bull. of A.A.U.P., XV, 1929.
Henderson, Y. and Davie, M., *Incomes and Living Costs of the University Faculty,* Yale Univ. Press, 1928.

Hill, David and Kelly, Fred, *Economy in Higher Education,* Carnegie Foundation, 1933.
Kelly, Fred and McNeely, John, *The State and Higher Education,* Carnegie Foundation, 1933.
MacCaughey, V., "Professors' Salaries," A Concise Bibliography, *School and Society,* VI, 535, 1917.
Peixotto, Jessica, *Getting and Spending at the Professional Standard of Living,* Macmillan, 1927.
Price, Richard, *The Financial Support of State Universities,* Harvard Univ. Press, 1924.
U. S. Office of Education, *Salary Trends in Private Colleges.*
U. S. Office of Education, "Salary Trends in Private Colleges," *School Life,* March, 1936.
U. S. Office of Education, "Salaries in Land-grant Colleges," Circular 157, February, 1936.
Veblen, Thorstein, *The Higher Learning in America,* Huebsch, 1918, Chapters 4 and 5.

PENSIONS

Cattell, James, *Carnegie Pensions,* Science Press, 1919.
Studensky, Paul, *Teachers' Pension Systems in the U. S.,* Appleton, 1920.
Carnegie Foundation for the Advancement of Teaching: Bulletins and Annual Reports.

ACADEMIC LIFE

Boas, George, *Never Go Back,* Harpers, 1926.
Canby, Henry, *Alma Mater,* op. cit., Chapter 6.
Herrick, Robert, *Chimes,* Macmillan, 1926.
Little, C. C., *The Awakening College,* Norton, 1930, Chapter 8.
Parker, James, *Academic Procession,* Harcourt Brace, 1937.

ACADEMIC FREEDOM

Bibliographies: Bull. of the A.A.U.P., XVIII, 399, 1932.
 Johnsen, Julia, *Academic Freedom,* Reference Shelf, III, No. 6, 1925.
 Johnsen, Julia, *Freedom of Speech,* Reference Shelf, X, No. 8, 1936.
American Civil Liberties Union, *The Gag on Teaching,* 1936.
Ashbrook, W., *The Organization and Activities of Boards Which Control Institutions of Higher Learning,* Unpub. Doctor's Thesis, Ohio State Univ., 1930.
Bates, Ernest, *This Land of Liberty,* Harper's, 1930, Chapter 12.
Beale, H. K., *Are American Teachers Free?,* Scribner's, 1936. A well-documented study of public-school teachers.
Bird, Joseph, *A Study of Faculty Control in State Universities in the U. S.,* Doctor's Thesis, New York Univ., 1930.
Bull. of the A.A.U.P., "Academic Freedom and Tenure," I, 1915. (Reprinted in same bulletin, October, 1937.)
Bull. of the A.A.U.P., "Place and Function of Faculties in University Government," X, 23-104, 1924.
Bull. of the A.A.U.P., "Faculty Participation in Administration," XXII, 512, 1936.
Bull. of the A.A.U.P., "Conference Statement of 1925," XXIV, 6, 1938.
Bull. of the A.A.U.P., "The Place and Function of Faculties in University and College Government," XXIV, 141, 1938.
Cattell, James, *University Control,* Science Press, 1913.

Cheyney, Edward, "Intellectual Freedom in a Democracy." Journal of Proceedings and Addresses of the Association of American Universities, November, 1936.

Cohen, David, *An Historical Analysis of the Problem of Academic Freedom of the Teacher in the Higher Institutions of Learning in the U. S. 1886-1933,* College of the City of New York, 1934.

Davis, Jerome, *Capitalism and Its Culture,* Farrar and Rinehart, 1935, Chapter 18.

Eliot, Charles, *University Administration,* Houghton Mifflin, 1908.

Elliott, E. C., Chambers, M. M., and Ashbrook, W. A., *The Government of Higher Education,* American Book Co., 1935. An account of documentary sources is appended.

Encyclopedia of the Social Sciences, I, "Academic Freedom."

Farrand, Livingston, "Code of Procedure of Governing Boards Regarding Appointments, Dismissal, and Tenure of University Teachers," National Association of State University Transactions, XIV, 205, 1916.

Flexner, Abraham, *Universities: American, English, German,* Oxford Univ. Press, 1930, pp. 178-86.

Gavit, John, *College,* Harcourt Brace, 1925, Chapter 9.

Hartshorne, Edward, *German Universities and National Socialism,* Harvard Press, 1937.

Hershey, Charles, *Historical Aspects of Church and Higher Education in the U. S.*

Hill, David, *Control of Tax-Supported Higher Education in the U. S.,* Carnegie Foundation, 1934.

Holme, E. R., *The American University, An Australian View,* Angus and Robertson, 1920, Chapter 2.

Hutchins, Robert, *No Friendly Voice,* Univ. of Chicago, 1936.

John Dewey Society (Second Yearbook), *Educational Freedom and Democracy,* Appleton Century, 1938.

Katzin, Samuel, *A Comparative Study of the Problem of Control in the Administration of Higher Education in the U. S. and Europe,* Doctor's Thesis, New York Univ., 1931.

Kent, Raymond, *Higher Education in America,* Ginn, 1930, Chapter 20.

Kirkpatrick, John, *The American College and its Rulers,* New Republic, 1926.

Kirkpatrick, John, *Academic Organization and Control,* Antioch Press, 1931.

Klapper, Paul, "The College Teacher and his Professional Status," *Educational Administration and Supervision,* XI, 73, 1925.

Lindsay, E. E., and Holland, E. O., *College and University Administration,* Macmillan, 1930.

Lippman, Walter, *American Inquisitors,* Macmillan, 1928.

Lundberg, Ferdinand, *America's 60 Families,* Vanguard Press, 1937, Chap. 10.

McNeely, John, "Authority of State Executive Agencies over Higher Education," U. S. Office of Education, Bulletin, 1936, No. 15.

Neilson, W. A., "Faculty Participation in University Government," Bull. of the A.A.U.P., XI, 156, 1925.

Raup, Bruce, *Education and Organized Interests in America,* G. P. Putnam's Sons, 1935.

Russell, J. D., and Reeves, F. W., *The Evaluation of Higher Institutions,* (Vol. 6, Administration), Univ. of Chicago, 1936, Chapter 2.

Schurman, J. G., "On the Satisfactory Experience of Cornell with Representation of the Faculty on the Board of Trustees," Bull. of the A.A.U.P., III, 9, 1917.

Sears, J. B., "Philanthropy in the History of American Higher Education," U. S. Office of Education, Bull. No. 26, 1922.

Sinclair, Upton, *The Goose Step*, 1923.

Sumner, William, *Folkways*, Ginn, 1906, Chapters 1 and 2.

Swift, Harold, "College and University as Seen by the Trustees," in *Obligations of Universities to the Social Order*, New York Univ. Press, 1933.

Thwing, C. F., *College President*, Macmillan, 1926.

Veblen, Thorstein, *The Higher Learning in America*, Huebsch, 1918.

TEACHING AND RESEARCH

Adams, Henry, *Education*, Houghton Mifflin, 1918, Chapter 20.

A.A.U.P., *College and University Teaching*, 1933.

Baldwin, T. W., "Normal Amount of Teaching and Research," Bull. of the A.A.U.P., XVI, 206, 1930.

Breed, F. S., "A Guide for College Teaching," *School and Society*, XXIV, 82, 1926.

Clinton, R. J., "Qualities College Students Desire in College Instructors," *School and Society*, XXXII, 702, 1930.

Crawford, C. C., "Defects and Difficulties in College Teaching," *School and Society*, XXVIII, 497, 1929.

Cross, W. L., "Improvement of College Teaching," Bull. of the Amer. Assn. of Colleges, XVI, 84, 1930.

Davis, C. O., "The Teaching Load in a University," *School and Society*, XIX, 556, 1924.

Good, Carter V., *Teaching in College and University*, Warwick and York, 1929. Exhaustive bibliography.

Johnston, John B., *The Liberal College in Changing Society*, Century, 1930, Chapter 14.

Judd, Chas. H., "Production of Good College Teaching," Bull. of the Assn. of American Colleges, XV, 90, 1929.

Kelly, R. L., "Great Teachers and Methods of Developing Them," Bull. of the Assn. of American Colleges, XV, 49, 1929.

Klapper, Paul, (ed.) *College Teaching*, World Book Co., 1920.

Laing, G. J., "The Doctor of Philosophy and College Teaching," Bull. of the American Assn. of Colleges, XVI, 95, 1930.

Little, C. C., *The Awakening College*, Norton, 1930, Chapter 8.

Marks, Percy, *Which Way Parnassus*, Harcourt Brace, 1926, Chapter 5.

Pace, Edward A., "Does Research Interfere with Teaching?" in Kelley, R. L. (ed.) *The Effective College*, Assn. of American Colleges, 1928.

Payne, Fernandus and Spieth, Evelyn, *An Open Letter to College Teachers*, Principia Press, 1935. Exhaustive bibliography.

Wriston, Henry, *The Nature of a Liberal College*, Lawrence College Press, 1937, Chapter 4.

POLITICAL AFFAIRS

War

Bull. of the A.A.U.P., IV, 29-47, 1918, "Academic Freedom in War-time."

Creel, George, *How We Advertised America*, Harper's, 1920, Chapter 8.

Kolbe, Parke R., *The Colleges in War-Time and After*, Appleton, 1919, Chapter 9.

Thwing, C. F., *American Colleges and Universities in the Great War*, Macmillan, 1920.

Brain Trust

Arnold, Thurman, *The Folklore of Capitalism,* Yale Press, 1937, Chapter 4.
Chapin, F. S., *Contemporary American Institutions,* Harper's, 1935, 146-149.
Obligation of Universities to the Social Order, N. Y. U. Press, 1933, Section III.

ANALYSIS AND INTERPRETATION

Bakeless, John, *Magazine Making,* Viking Press, 1931.
Gray, W. S., and Munroe, Ruth, *The Reading Interests and Habits of Adults,* Macmillan, 1930.
Hart, Hornell, "Changing Opinions about Business Prosperity: A Consensus of Magazine Opinion in the U. S. 1929-32," *Amer. Journ. of Sociology,* XXXVIII, 665, 1933.
Hart, Hornell, "Changing Social Attitudes and Interests," in *Recent Social Trends,* McGraw Hill, 1933, Chapter 8.
Lundberg, G. A., "The Newspaper and Public Opinion," *Social Forces,* IV, 709, 1926.

MAGAZINES

Drewry, John E., *Some Magazines and Magazine Makers,* Stratford, 1924.
Howe, Mark A. D., *Atlantic Monthly and Its Makers,* Atlantic Monthly Press, 1919.
Mott, Frank L., *American Magazines,* 1865-1880, Midland Press, 1928.
Pollak, Gustav, *Fifty Years of American Idealism,* Houghton Mifflin, 1915, (History of the *Nation,* 1865-1915.)
Tassin, Algernon, *The Magazine in America,* Dodd, Mead, 1916. (History of magazines until the close of the nineteenth century.)
Ayer, N. W. and Son, *Directory of Newspapers and Periodicals,* Annual volumes.

INDEX

The Academic Profession

An Arno Press Collection

Annan, Noel Gilroy. **Leslie Stephen:** His Thought and Character in Relation to His Time. 1952

Armytage, W. H. G. **Civic Universities:** Aspects of a British Tradition. 1955

Berdahl, Robert O. **British Universities and the State.** 1959

Bleuel, Hans Peter. **Deutschlands Bekenner** (German Men of Knowledge). 1968

Bowman, Claude Charleton. **The College Professor in America.** 1938

Busch, Alexander. **Die Geschichte des Privatdozenten** (History of Privat-Docentens). 1959

Caplow, Theodore and Reece J. McGee. **The Academic Marketplace.** 1958

Carnegie Foundation for the Advancement of Teaching. **The Financial Status of the Professor in America and in Germany.** 1908

Cattell, J. McKeen. **University Control.** 1913

Cheyney, Edward Potts. **History of the University of Pennsylvania:** 1740-1940. 1940

Elliott, Orrin Leslie. **Stanford University:** The First Twenty-Five Years. 1937

Ely, Richard T. **Ground Under Our Feet:** An Autobiography. 1938

Flach, Johannes. **Der Deutsche Professor der Gegenwart** (The German Professor Today). 1886

Hall, G. Stanley. **Life and Confessions of a Psychologist.** 1924

Hardy, G[odfrey] H[arold]. **Bertrand Russell & Trinity:** A College Controversy of the Last War. 1942

Kluge, Alexander. **Die Universitäts-Selbstverwaltung** (University Self-Government). 1958

Kotschnig, Walter M. **Unemployment in the Learned Professions.** 1937

Lazarsfeld, Paul F. and Wagner Thielens, Jr. **The Academic Mind:** Social Scientists in a Time of Crisis. 1958

McLaughlin, Mary Martin. **Intellectual Freedom and Its Limitations in the University of Paris in the Thirteenth and Fourteenth Centuries.** 1977

Metzger, Walter P., editor. **The American Concept of Academic Freedom in Formation:** A Collection of Essays and Reports. 1977

Metzger, Walter P., editor. **The Constitutional Status of Academic Freedom.** 1977

Metzger, Walter P., editor. **The Constitutional Status of Academic Tenure.** 1977

Metzger, Walter P., editor. **Professors on Guard:** The First AAUP Investigations. 1977

Metzger, Walter P., editor. **Reader on the Sociology of the Academic Profession.** 1977

Mims, Edwin. **History of Vanderbilt University.** 1946

Neumann, Franz L., et al. **The Cultural Migration:** The European Scholar in America. 1953

Nitsch, Wolfgang, et al. **Hochschule in der Demokratie** (The University in a Democracy). 1965

Pattison, Mark. **Suggestions on Academical Organization with Especial Reference to Oxford.** 1868

Pollard, Lucille Addison. **Women on College and University Faculties:** A Historical Survey and a Study of Their Present Academic Status. 1977

Proctor, Mortimer R. **The English University Novel.** 1957

Quincy, Josiah. **The History of Harvard University.** Two vols. 1840

Ross, Edward Alsworth. **Seventy Years of It:** An Autobiography. 1936

Rudy, S. Willis. **The College of the City of New York:** A History, 1847-1947. 1949

Slosson, Edwin E. **Great American Universities.** 1910

Smith, Goldwin. **A Plea for the Abolition of Tests in the University of Oxford.** 1864

Willey, Malcolm W. **Depression, Recovery and Higher Education:** A Report by Committee Y of the American Association of University Professors. 1937

Winstanley, D. A. **Early Victorian Cambridge.** 1940

Winstanley, D. A. **Later Victorian Cambridge.** 1947

Winstanley, D. A. **Unreformed Cambridge.** 1935

Yeomans, Henry Aaron. **Abbott Lawrence Lowell: 1856-1943.** 1948